Heart For The Lost

Rudy Waters

Heart for the Lost

Codex Spiritualis Press
Printed in the United States of America.
ISBN: 9798720640903

Library of Congress data is available for this title.

Endorsements

"I've known Rudy Waters and his family personally for years. He is a man of conviction, sensitivity, and high character. He has a genuine love for the lost and for the poor.

He is also among the rare breed of evangelists God is raising up today that not only inspires the Church to win the lost, but is an example of it and equips believers to do it themselves.

When my wife and I were missionaries years ago we had a methodology of discipleship that was ingrained into our team: *"What people only hear they soon forget. What they see, they tend to remember. But it's what they do that they understand."* This is how Rudy works as an evangelist. He disciples the believer in evangelism and working in the harvest fields.

I encourage every pastor to invite Rudy to equip your church in evangelism.

-Bert M. Farias, Holy Fire Ministries

Windham, NH

"Rudy Waters is one of the purest and most authentic soul winners I know. In a generation where so many have been seduced by the glamor of professional ministry, Rudy is still reaching into the darkness to rescue the least, the last, and the lost. His life is laid down, a living martyr. The kind of man of which the world is not worthy. I look forward to the day I am able to celebrate with my friend the great "Well done." Until that day there is much work to be done, and much we can learn from faithful laborers like Rudy Waters."

- Evangelist Levi Lutz, Together in the Harvest Ministries

Orlando, Fl.

"Evangelist Rudy Waters is seriously used by God both in the United States and abroad to spread the good news of Jesus and revival to the lost and found alike. For the last few years, knowing him and his family has helped to spiritually transform our family, ministry, business, and the city of Tuscaloosa and on a personal level. Knowing him, his wife Tami, and his son John has been a great blessing to all of us. With a pure heart, Rudy has been a great blessing to all of us. I have watched him personally up close to get to know his heart. I believe strongly in who he is, what he does for the kingdom of God, and what the Lord has chosen Rudy to do. As one of his board members of Go and Declare, Inc. I strongly support him!"

-Pastor Abraham Israel Javine,

New Rehoboth International Family Church & Tuscaloosa International Prayer Center

"I have known Rudy Waters for almost 20 years, and we have spent the last seven years traveling and ministering together around America and the Nations. There is no purer heart when talking about Rudy and evangelism than his. He honestly does not care about being noticed or having a big name in man's eyes. He truly wants every person to come to the knowledge of Christ. He is a true evangelist in all matters of speaking, so I encourage everyone to read this book. It will change your life and allow this humble servant to teach you things that God has taught him concerning evangelism and walking with Jesus."

-Missionary/Evangelist Richard Davis Heart of Asia Ministries

Birmingham, Alabama

"I did not even know what an evangelist was until I met Rudy Waters. He is a purebred soul winner. His words will inspire you to reach out to the broken, the hurting, and take your place at the plow in the master's great harvest field."

-Evangelist Jon Hale, Harvest Now Ministries

"Rudy is a dear friend. We have been close and ministered together for many years. I met him on my first trip to Kumba, Cameroon. He is an intense soul-winner and equipping evangelist. He knows how to bring lost souls into the kingdom of God through miracle evangelism."

-Evangelist Joel Crumpton, Broken Pieces Outreach Ministries

Contents

Introduction

You are about to read a true story of my broken life that an amazing Holy God changed. A tale of an amazing God that rescued me from destruction and healed every part of my heart. He would take this broken heart, put it back together, replace it with His love and send me out to rescue others that had broken lives. To share my story, the Lord would have me go all the way back to when I was at a young age.

The enemy hates us and wants to destroy our lives early. I believe he is scared of what we will do for God and immediately tries to steal the seed of our lives once we enter the world. The enemy comes to steal, kill, and destroy, but the Lord brings life more abundantly.

You will read some of my life history and how the Lord rescued me. Then, I share many things I have learned since I was born again and baptized in the Holy Ghost. The Lord has blessed me with so many mentors and teachers in my life. It is an honor to share what I have learned from them and what the Holy Spirit has taught me.

My favorite part is all the evangelism methods that I have learned, and it is an honor to share them with you. I think of them like Batman's utility belt, full of many components for handling whatever situations that arise. We can lean on the Holy Spirit to use the right tools at the precise time when we need them.

I pray the Holy Spirit will radically change your life as you read the pages of this book. I believe you will never be the same, and it will give you hunger in your heart for lost souls. May you get the heart of the Father and bring everyone you can to the Marriage Supper of the Lamb. It is going to be glorious!

Chapter 1

My Early Life

Oh, To Be A Child, Again

I believe the Lord marked me at a young age. My parents used to go to a Presbyterian Church, and throughout my life, they told me that I stood up in front of the church and sang "Jesus Loves Me-Yes, I Know for the Bible Tells Me So". It must have been a precious time for my Mom because she would talk about it often. She would say how wonderful it was when I was singing it. When I reflect on this childhood memory, I consider the greatness of the love of our heavenly Father. He must have soaked in all that praise. A little child singing about how much God loves Him must have been a sweet-smelling fragrance to the Lord.

I think about what Jesus said in Matthew 18:2-4 "*Then Jesus called a small child to Him, set him in the midst of them, and said, 'Assuredly, I say to you, unless you are converted and become as little children, you will by no means enter the kingdom of Heaven. Therefore, whoever humbles himself as this small child is the greatest in the realm of Heaven.*"

I believe I was around three years old at the time, and innocent from the ways of the world. My parents had not divorced yet, and I think it was one of my most beautiful days on the earth.

Oh, to sing praises to our King. Oh, how the smell of the fragrance must have been to Him. I think of how He must have felt turning and looking around. Bragging with the angels saying there is one of my children singing about how much He loves me. All of heaven must have chimed in singing along about the love of Jesus. What a moment that must have been. Oh, to be a little child again!

Not only was I marked by the Lord, but I believe the enemy knew of the calling on my life and tried to destroy me early on. He had attacked my parents, and they ended up divorcing when I was around five years old. My dad was an alcoholic his whole life, and he was very violent towards my mom. I remember them fighting all the time and my mom screaming because of him beating her.

This one time stuck with me all my life. I was around five years old at the time. My father had come to the house, and my mom would not let him in. He had opened the door, but he could not get in because of the chain lock. I remember seeing him peek in through the door. There was so much anger on his face. He started bashing the door in, and everyone in the house was frantic. My brother, sister, and I ran to hide. I remember hearing my mom screaming frantically, and there was nothing I could do, I thought. I was in a state of fear, hiding in a dark room, thinking to myself, what can I do? What can a five-year-old do?

I looked and saw the telephone in the dark room that I was hiding in and immediately jumped on the phone. My mom had taught me to dial 911 for the police. I got the police operator on the phone. I was quiet and tried to whisper what was happening. Suddenly the phone went dead, and there was nothing but a dial tone.

My father had pulled out the telephone cord and then walked out of the room. I was still in fear. Oh, no, I thought, but it was quiet. I decided to sneak out of the room and look, and I saw this huge man. He was a New York State Trooper that had come to our rescue. He was a mountain of a man compared to my dad. In an instant, my dad became very humble. Everything calmed down, and my dad left. We were all thankful because it could have been a lot worse.

I believe that the enemy was trying to destroy my dad with alcohol, and he pretty much succeeded because he suffered from this addiction his whole life. Not only did the enemy destroy my dad's life, but for many years it affected his kids. To this day, still, some of us struggle with the addiction of alcohol, and the only way out for me was to turn my focus on the Deliverer, King Jesus.

It was not all bad. There were times when my dad was a fantastic person. After the divorce with my mom, he would remarry and have two girls, my two half-sisters Cassie and Mandy. I remember my sister Tammy and brother Mark and I would be so happy when he would come and pick us up on weekends. My dad was so much fun. He was a practical joker, and he would take us camping all the time.

Our weekends were terrific, and we got to spend them with our new sisters. We could only see them on the weekends, making it so unique. I still remember a guitar being there, and I would act goofy trying to play it. It was a special time in my life. I loved playing with my half-sisters. I was no longer the youngest, and I loved them so much!

Like I said, I remember grabbing this guitar and acting silly with it. I believe I got my sense of humor from my dad because he liked to goof around most of the time and would play practical jokes on folks. I love to remember those times instead of the bad ones.

My mom would meet a man named Bill and remarry as well. When my mom would date, us kids would always plan to run the guy off. It was usually my brother Mark's idea, and my sister and I would typically go along with it. I remember Bill came to eat dinner with us, and my brother had taken all the screws out of his chair. Bill sat in the chair, and *BAM*, he went straight to the floor.

We couldn't understand why that didn't run him off, but Bill just kept coming back for more. He loved my mom, and he was willing to put up with us rambunctious kids, and I believe he grew to love us, as well.

After the wedding, our house on Garlow Road in the Town of Wheatfield, NY, was sold. I was around ten years old at the time. I had no idea what was going to happen. My world was about to change. I had no idea.

I had just gotten back from a beautiful trip to Kentucky with my father's family. I had terrific relatives in Kentucky. My Grandmother, Dori Waters, was so amazing. When we would go, it would always smell like fantastic food, and the biscuits in gravy were so delicious. I did not see my family there very often, but everyone was so full of love for Tammy, Mark, and I. I still remember to this day my grandmother always telling me how much she loved me.

While on this Kentucky trip, I observed that my father was given a piece of property, and while we were there, he started to build his home. I had no idea that this would be the home where my father and his new family would live for the rest of his life. I didn't realize that when our vacation was over, my father would take Tammy, Mark, and I back to Niagara Falls, NY, to be with my mom, and I would see him no more until I was in my twenties.

Moving Into The City

Bill and my mom married, and we were moving into the city of Niagara Falls. I had to tell all my friends that I would have to move. It was extremely hard for me having to say goodbye to all my friends. For around ten years, that was all I knew, and it was unfortunate to leave all of them. I was about to walk into a new city and a new home. Because my mom had remarried, we had sold our house.

We used the money from the sale to purchase my stepfathers' old home in the Lasalle area of Niagara Falls, New York. I remember feeling all the pain of my father's lack of communication, not seeing my sisters anymore, and leaving everything I knew. I had to go to a new school, make new friends, and had no idea what was about to happen.

My stepfather had two children of his own. I had met them a few times, and now my sister, brother, and I were about to move into a new home with my stepsister and stepbrother. I had no problems with my stepsister. She was pretty and she was kind to me which I appreciated.

On the other hand, I had now received another older brother. As I said, I would no longer see my half-sisters anymore, and now I received another older brother. I was usually picked on a lot by my older brothers, but it wasn't all bad. I never really had to fight anyone in school because both my older brothers were tough, and the kids just assumed that I could beat them up, or if they picked on me, they were afraid they would have to deal with my older brothers.

The pain of missing my father continued, and the change affected me. Halfway through fifth grade, I contracted mononucleosis and spent time in the hospital. I loved receiving all the attention from the doctors, nurses, and family. I did not want that to end, so after getting home from the hospital. I decided to come up with a plan that I could not walk.

Everyone believed that I was too weak to walk from the mono, and it went on for an exceedingly long time. I think I went back to the hospital and started receiving all the attention again. The doctors used electricity to shock my legs, and I could feel the electricity; they concluded that my problem was not physical but mental. I would then have to see a psychiatrist.

I am sure this situation must have been costing my mom and stepfather a lot of money. My mom would take me up to her room and through fear and intimidation, brought me out of it. I still remember it to this day, seeing the anger on her face when she would shake me and yell at me, telling me that I could walk and that it was all in my head.

My mom had been through a rough time, and I do not fault her for the situation. I had started believing that I could not walk. You see, if you tell a lie long enough, you even start thinking it is true yourself. I started accepting it and my mom helped me out of it. I came down from that room walking and went back to school soon after.

My family did not talk about what happened from that point on. I had it buried in my heart. I had no idea how much pain I was in, but I would carry a deep wound for many years. I had it so buried in my heart that when some of my family would ask me if I remembered what had happened, I would just say I don't remember. The Holy Spirit would bring it up to the surface many years later and after I gave my life to the Lord, I received healing from it. Thank You, Jesus, for healing me!

I started getting more and more into drugs and alcohol in my teen years and I decided to join a fraternity called Gamma Sigma in High School. Most folks would call me a burnout in school, but I was determined to get good grades for some reason. My parents had motivated my brother to graduate high school by giving him a shotgun, and they used the same tactic on me.

They had promised to help me pay for a used car, and it worked, but my life would still be a complete wreck, mostly in secret. The fraternity would have parties all the time, and I would come home drunk and high pretty much every night, even on weekdays. Often, I would wake up in the morning and have no idea how I got home. I believe the Lord's hand was on me and that someone was praying for me. Thank You, Lord, for your mercy.

Hazing Almost Leads To 3-5 Years In Jail

In my senior year, I had become president of the fraternity. Hazing was a big part of our initiation into the club. We would take bats and shave them down to be a paddle. We would also have a big paddle placed over the person's tail bone while paddling them. We would have future members pledge for months for their initiation night. They would have to carry a black notebook with merits and demerits in them. If you did well, you would not get paddled as hard. One night in September of 1985, we had two teenagers paddled so hard that they had to go to the hospital with internal bleeding. Our fraternity was all over the news including a feature story on Good Morning America.

We were in huge trouble, and I was the president. We conducted a meeting and decided to say that we had not elected officers yet. That scheme did not work. In a couple of days, my treasurer and I would be at the police station for questioning. The detective had called my mom. She had already told the officer that I was the president, and I was guilty. My treasurer and I would have to give written statements and later have a whole fraternity meeting. It turned out that the parents did not press charges on us, and we got off with a warning. It was a wake-up call. I do not believe our fraternity had any more initiations that year.

Looking back on it, I believe the Lord used some of it for good. Being the president of the fraternity, I learned leadership skills. I had to conduct meetings, help lead the officers and keep everyone in unity. I was amazed by the agreement of our fraternity. I remember another fraternity challenging us to a football game, and the loser would have to buy a keg of beer.

We took the challenge knowing that we had no money in our treasury for a keg of beer. It was either win the game or rumble (that is what we call a fraternity fight back then, it's more of a gang term). Our fraternity practiced pretty much every day we could. We were desperate to win the game, and nobody would stop us. We would end up winning the game 51-0. Sigma Psi bought us our keg of beer that evening, and we all had a party that night. Little did I know the Lord was raising a leader and would use me to lead folks to build up His Kingdom later.

After high school, I had received a job working for a pizza place called La Hacienda in Niagara Falls, New York. I started making a living for myself and got more into the dating scene. I continued with the drugs, alcohol, and sexual sin entered my life. I would work late nights, go out to bars, and pretty much come home when the sun came up. That lifestyle affected my college career. I only made it through half of a semester, and I quit pretty much satisfied with my life working in the restaurant scene. I went from job to job, girlfriend to girlfriend, and more drugs and more alcohol.

In my twenties, I started working at a Best Western Restaurant, and I met a girl there that I would date for most of my mid-twenties. We would begin living together as if we were married. That was a big mistake because there was no commitment, especially on her side. I had gotten out of restaurant work and took a job at a lumber yard. I had to work late-night shifts. I started sensing something was going on.

My girlfriend started cheating on me with her mechanic. One night I ended up getting out of work early and came home. She was not home yet, and while I was there, her mechanic dropped her off. I decided to take my belongings and go live with my brother. That lasted like one night. She followed me to my brothers that night, and we reconciled with me moving back in. I should have taken the hint that she was an unfaithful person, but I did not. I would go down more of a road of sin and frustration, but I believe the Lord led me in some strange way. He was taking something meant for evil to turn it around for good!

In the Fall of 1990, I was ecstatic to have an opportunity to move to Ocala, Florida. It was an opportunity to get out of the snow and make a new life for myself. I was living in Niagara Falls, New York, and I was tired of the cold winters. To be honest, the only thing I loved about Western New York was my football team, the Buffalo Bills, which I still watch and love to this day. I had no idea that the Lord was setting me up. He was getting me away from most of my party friends, and eventually, I would run smack dab into the Valley of Decision.

So, in the Fall of 1990, my girlfriend and I would move to Ocala, Florida, to get jobs and live with my parents for a couple of years until we decided to get our own Mobile Home. I had proposed to her and given her a ring, but she had given no promise of marriage. The only thing I got was a maybe. I should have taken the hint because my world would change very soon. My life would never be the same after what was about to happen and would lead to me sharing my testimony with hundreds of people and possibly thou-

sands after this book is published. Here it is!

Chapter 2

My Personal Testimony

Betrayed! My Girlfriend Was Living With Another Man In My Home!

I suspected that she was cheating on me. She stayed out all night partying with her "friends from work" then coming home either drunk or hungover. She seemed to be interested in this new guy at work. I confronted her and demanded to know if she was having an affair. She lied to me and denied it. I was furious. I stormed out of the home in a jealous rage, slamming the door behind me. I left and moved to my parent's house nearby. How could she do this to me? We had lived together for five years, and I loved this girl. I had offered to marry her. Didn't that mean anything to her? What about all the good times we had shared?

I had not been the best guy to hang around, to be honest. I was a regular drinker. I had not always been considerate of her. Maybe we could talk this out, I reasoned. A week later, I found out that the guy from work had moved in with her. I was outraged! I called her on the phone. She still denied having an affair. She insisted that this man she was now living with was "just a friend." Yeah, right. She said that she "didn't want me out of the picture yet." What did that mean? I could feel my rage boiling over. I threatened to kill her and her new lover. I slammed down the receiver.

One of my buddies at work tried to console me. "Forget about her. You'll find another one." He took me to bars, but it did not help. I really could not talk to any women. I was angry with all women because of what my girlfriend had done to me. I became depressed and tried to fill my life up with pornography. My thoughts became darker, and I contemplated suicide.

One day I was sitting in front of the television channel surfing, and I stopped and heard a pastor preaching a sermon on forgiveness. His speech was about forgiving others so God could forgive us. He said that God could not forgive us unless we forgive others. He read a scripture from the book of Mark. "If you do not forgive, neither will your Father in heaven forgive you your trespasses." I realized that I was a sinner and needed forgiveness for my sins.

I also realized that I needed to forgive my ex-girlfriend for what she did to me. The pastor prayed a prayer of salvation, and I accepted Jesus into my heart. When I got up from my knees praying,

I felt the load of sin and depression lift from me. The Lord had given me peace. A peace that I had never had before. I felt God's, unconditional love. God had sacrificed Jesus, His only Son, for me. Jesus willingly died on the cross and took the punishment I had deserved so that I could have abundant life, and when I die, He has a place for me in Heaven. Even when I did not know God, He still loved me. If I had been the only person on earth, God always would have sent Jesus to die for me. And that would be the same for you. He did it for all of us.

Do you need peace? Maybe you are not struggling with loneliness, anger, or depression-like I was. Whatever it is that you are fighting against, Jesus is the answer. He can help you overcome anything. Are you sick? Jesus is the healer. Are you addicted to pornography, drugs, or alcohol? Jesus will set you free.

God loves you and has an excellent plan for your life. The Bible says in Jeremiah 29:11, "*For I know the thoughts I think toward you, says the Lord, thoughts of peace and not of evil, to give you a hope and a future.*"

Jesus said in John 10:10, "*I have come that they may have life and have it more abundantly.*"

How Can You Receive The Abundant Life Jesus Has For You?

In John 3:3, Jesus said to Nicodemus, a religious leader, *"Unless one is born again, he cannot see the kingdom,"* In Romans 10:9-10, the Bible says, *"That if you confess with your mouth the Lord Jesus and believe in your heart that God raised Him from the dead, you will be saved. For with the heart, one believes unto righteousness; and with the mouth, confession is made unto salvation."*

If you confess with your mouth and believe in your heart that Jesus is the Son of God and that He died for your sins and rose again, you can be assured that you will go to Heaven.

Pray This Prayer:

Dear God, I know that I have sinned and need help. I believe in my heart that Jesus is your Son, that He died on the cross for my sins, and that You raised Him from the dead. Jesus, I ask for your forgiveness of my sins; wash me clean with your blood. Jesus, I open my heart and invite you to come in. Make yourself real to me. I confess you as Lord and Savior in my life. Please help me to walk with You and learn Your ways. I give You total control of my life. Amen.

Where do I go from here?

Pray every day. Read your Bible, beginning with the New Testament. Attend a good Bible-believing church that operates in the Holy Spirit's gifts and teaches the whole gospel of Jesus Christ. Receive full-immersion baptism. Fellowship regularly with other believers in Jesus Christ.

Chapter 3

God Wins

The Thief Came To Steal, Kill And Destroy

I remember the devil tried to kill me many times throughout my childhood. He was afraid of the calling of God on my life and tried to snuff me out early. I was sitting with a friend on our pool deck the first time. My friend pushed me into the pool. I could not swim, and I remember sitting at the pool's bottom drowning. My sister Tammy looked out the back door and saw that I was no longer sitting on the deck. She ran as fast as she could and jumped into the water to save me. It was just in time! Praise God the enemy lost that one.

Another time was when I was fishing on a dock at our cottage in Canada. It is a funny story today, but it was not funny back then. I went to cast my line out, but I shot myself into the water, and my pole stayed on the dock. I still had not learned to swim yet, so I grabbed hold of the edge of the dock with my hands. I held on for dear life, and it seemed like I was there for an eternity. I could feel my little hands slipping as I cried out for help! Had I let go, I probably would not be here today! Praise God, He had another plan! My Aunt Libby heard me screaming, and she saw my little hands hanging on at the end of the dock. Praise God! I was rescued and lived to see another day.

The third time, I was playing with my friends in the street. A car came by us on the road, and we got out of the way. Immediately a couple of guys jumped out of the car and asked us if we wanted to go for a ride. Praise God we kept our distance and remembered that our parents taught us to stay away from strangers.

These guys started screaming in rage for us to get in the car! I remember fear gripping my heart! We started running as the men chased us in their car. We got away by running through our neighbors' yards. Who knows what those men would have done to us had they caught us? I do not believe I would be alive today to tell you the story if we had been kidnapped that day. The devil lost again!

Many times, the enemy tried to kill me. I do not know how many times I should have been dead and in hell through my teens and twenties, but God had a plan. Drugs, alcohol, and riotous living could have taken me out. I believe the Lord was using folks to pray for me. I do not know who, but I praise God for them. The Lord has a plan, and He calls intercessors to pray even if they are in another country. Someone prayed for me, and I thank God for them. I believe I will meet them in eternity and get a chance to thank them!

But Jesus Came To Bring Life And More Abundantly

I was twenty-seven when I was born again. Everything changed! Although I could not do drugs anymore because of random drug testing at my job, my alcohol consumption had tripled, but once I was born again, I was immediately set free. I stopped listening to Ozzy Osbourne and Rock and Roll and listened to the Christian Radio Station instead. The Lord had pursued me my whole life, and I finally gave in; there was no going back. When I went to work the next day, the guys were shocked. I walked in with so much peace and joy in my life. I started witnessing to them right away. Most of them would pretty much stay away from me, but the Lord would use me for a season there, and a couple of guys gave their life to Jesus. Praise God!

I had put off going to church long enough, so I set out on a quest to find where the Lord wanted me. The first Sunday, I walked into a Methodist Church. The people were genuinely friendly, and the service was good, but I knew in my heart that this was not the church for me.

In Ocala, I worked at a van conversion company called Mark III. I knew a guy that looked like Samson. He had big arms and long hair, and I knew he was a Christian because he would talk about Jesus all the time. I asked him if he knew of any good churches, and he told me about his church called the Church of God that had a "Grads" singles class for people who were college aged. I was single, so it sparked my curiosity. I thought, well, maybe my wife might be there. The Lord was going to set me up again!

I could not get his recommendation to go to this Church of God out of my head. I walked into the service, and I could feel something different about it. A presence I never felt before. I thought this is nothing like the churches I grew up in back home. The worship was amazing, and I saw folks lifting their hands to the Lord. I thought this church is weird, but I continued to go back because of my curiosity.

The minister got up to speak, and it was mass chaos, I thought. I cannot remember the message, but he was charismatic and energized. Folks were running around praising the Lord, and I heard folks praying in various languages and running to the altar to pray. They believed in the Lord for revival. I listened to a whisper in my ear that I now know was from the enemy. He said these people are weird, and you do not need to be in this church. You need to get out of here now, so I left, but deep inside my heart, I wanted what they had.

In the morning, I went back to work with all kinds of questions for my friend. I had so much curiosity. I wanted to know what in the world was going on in that church. He explained that every-thing that was going on was in the Bible and encouraged me to read it in the Book of Acts. He then encouraged me to give it one more visit and reminded me of the Grads singles class again.

Chapter 4

Receiving the Holy Ghost and Learning to Pray

My First Encounter With The Holy Ghost

I was so intrigued with going to this singles class that I had to go that Sunday. I walked into the church and asked the first person I could see to direct me to the classroom. I thought maybe there was a good Christian girl there that I could meet to be my future wife. I walked in and met this fantastic couple. There was something different about them. They were prayer people and knew how to tap into hearing from the Lord.

Rhonda was a prophetic intercessor, and she started teaching. I was getting lightheaded in my seat. To be honest, I thought I was going to pass out. I did not hear much that she had to say that day because I was drunk in the Holy Spirit and didn't know it. In the end, folks would ask me if I was alright, and I said yes, not wanting to embarrass myself.

I got up, staggering to the sanctuary for the service, and it was a lot like the week before. The Lord would move powerfully that day! I would start listening to a distinct voice, the Holy Ghost. There was no turning back, the enemy lost that battle, and I am glad he did.

Receiving The Power Of The Holy Ghost

I remember responding to an altar call one Sunday evening at the Church of God that I was now attending. Several men were standing there and surrounded me to pray for me. I cannot remember everything they prayed, but I remember feeling warm inside and experiencing so much peace. The gentlemen started praying for me to receive the Holy Ghost's Baptism. One of the men started coaching me and had me open my mouth to utter some easy words to say that were not in English. I took off! I started just using my tongue by saying la, la, and then I remember the presence of God getting stronger. I could no longer stand as one of the men prophesied over me about being a prophet.

I did not understand that at all and still do not. Maybe that is still in the future. After the meeting that night, I went home and got alone in my room. I was very intrigued by what had just happened to me. Was this just a one-time experience, or could this be a gift? Of course, the devil was lying to me, telling me that I received nothing. I closed my bedroom door, and I remember saying, OK Lord, if this is Your gift, I will do it. I opened my mouth and started to utter the words that were easiest to say. The Holy Spirit's presence came on me, and it was as if there was a person that just entered the room. Well, a person had entered the room for sure He was the person of the Holy Ghost. I got scared and stopped praying, but all I could feel was perfect peace, so I did it again and again. The Holy Spirit was teaching me how to pray and as I practiced, he was giving me more and more words to say. He was teaching me. You see, I learned later that a bodybuilder never starts with heavyweights. He starts with small ones and then works his way up to heavier weights. That is what the Holy Spirit was doing to me. I started with minimal language, but today the Lord has given me a complete language of tongues, and it is glorious. Praise Jesus! He gave me the gift to pray His perfect will, and later, He would tell me that all the other gifts would come out of praying in the Holy Ghost!

Learning To Pray And The Gift Of Intercession

After receiving the gift of the Holy Spirit, I had this hunger in my heart to learn how to pray. The Lord had set me up. In the class that I was going to, the teacher was a prophetic intercessor. I was intrigued by her prayer life and desired what she had. She would always get scriptures on her heart, hear from God, and would flow with what was on God's heart. I made sure to be in every one of her classes, and if she had functions outside of the church, I would be there.

The Lord was using her to disciple me. She poured the word of God into me, and I found myself hearing from God. As I spent time with Him, the Lord would share with me what was on His heart. The Lord was using this precious lady to disciple me and put the word of God into my life. There is not a day that goes by that I do not think about the price Rhonda paid to pour into us in that Grads Sunday School Class. I know she will receive a huge reward in heaven for this! God Bless you, Rhonda! I love you!

Demon Possessed Girl

I will never forget what happened! I was still a young Christian and newly filled with the Holy Ghost. Many people brought this young girl into our Sunday School Class after it was over. They surrounded her and began to pray. This girl's eyes started twitching and rolling back into her head. She then started speaking in a man's voice, saying, "I am not Angie." I was like, this is crazy, but I wanted to stay in there to see what was about to happen. Folks that had not received the Holy Ghost were required to leave the room. I thought, well, I just got the Holy Ghost, so I am OK, and I stayed.

They wrestled with this lady for a long time. I believe it was for around an hour. They spoke to that demon to come out of her. She was throwing people around as if she was a bodybuilder. It took several men to keep her steady. Finally, she was free, and all the demons had left. I thought to myself; this is the real deal! That night gave me so much confirmation that God and the Devil were real. There was no going back now!

Chapter 5

Revival and Getting Married

Hunger For Revival

My Sunday School teachers and our church would always talk about revival. I remember them sharing with me about a revivalist that had obeyed the Lord to come to America. The Lord had started moving powerfully in the meetings, usually with laughter and folks feeling drunk in the Holy Spirit.

They shared a video with us and what was happening in the video started happening to us while we were watching it. I thought to myself, I need to get some of that. The opportunity came, and our teachers took us to one of the meetings. I was so excited but had no idea what was going to happen. Pastor Rodney got up to preach and the joy of the Lord moved like waves across the sanctuary.

Folks started getting drunk in the Holy Spirit, and they could not stand anymore as they would fall to the ground. I thought this is amazing! Pastor Rodney would have everyone line up for prayer. When he came to pray for me, I immediately fell down to the ground. I was on the ground next to this precious lady who was probably in her eighties, and holy laughter hit me. I was laughing hysterically! I remember not being able to get up from the floor. Looking over to the right, the precious lady next to me was experiencing the same thing. She was stuck to the floor, laughing hysterically, and told me that she could not get up.

What a meeting! I remember us driving back to Ocala that night having a fantastic time with the Lord. We decided to share the testimonies with our class the next morning. Revival broke out in our Sunday School. Everyone was laughing hysterically and was drunk in the Holy Spirit. I do not even believe we made it into the sanctuary for our service that day.

We had revival right there. That meeting gave me so much hunger for the presence of God and revival. I was changed and received a burden that has never left me. The Lord became so real to me. I wanted everyone to experience everything that I was experiencing.

Hunger For More Revival

The hunger for more of God continued. I went to my Sunday School teacher's house for a prayer meeting, and she shared with us a video from a revival that had broken out on Father's Day of 1995. It was already the Summer of 1996, and the revival had been going on for over a year.

In the video, I saw two girls give their testimony. One of the girls was shaking uncontrollably! I remember myself getting closer to the television and feeling the presence of God as she shared. I said to myself, that I needed to get out there to receive that power-ful presence of God.

Within a week, a couple of friends and I planned a trip to Pen-sacola, Florida, where the revival was at Brownsville Assembly of God Church. We drove all night to get there, and we got there ear-ly in the morning to get in line. Hungry people were already there waiting. We got in line, and the line would get longer and longer throughout the day.

People had come from all over the world. The presence of God was wonderful even while we waited. Folks would be worshipping and praying throughout the day. There was so much hunger from these people that it was contagious. I thought to myself, what will it be like when I get inside the church? My anticipation had grown, and I could not wait for the service. Finally, the time had come. A wonderful African American man who served on security started letting people in the church. He would scream out, "single-file line, no backpacks, watch your step folks, watch your step!" I was so excited to be going in finally.

Thousands of hungry people were going into worship Jesus! Lindell Cooley and the Worship Team came in, and as soon he hit the keys, it was like a bomb went off. A rumbling of praise and worship to the Lord had erupted! The building shook. Earlier during the announcements, they warned the balcony folks not to jump up and down on the balcony because it could collapse.

The people disregarded the warning, and there were hundreds of people jumping up and down in extravagant worship. It was awesome, but it sounded and shook as if an earthquake was happening. I thought to myself, this must be a glimpse of what heaven must be, and I wanted everything God had for me, so I pressed in worshipping Jesus.

After worship, a man named Steve Hill got up to preach. I had never heard anyone preach like this before. He was earnest about lost souls and preached a very confronting message on sin and giving your life one hundred percent to the Lord. I will never forget him saying, "if you don't wake up in the morning with Jesus on your lips or go to bed with Jesus on your lips, I question your salvation?" I started feeling convicted in my heart and ran to the altar giving everything to Jesus. I had no idea that my life would change forever. I believe that running to Jesus was the beginning of the call on my life to give everything to Him and bring in the lost. The Lord changed me in a moment.

Radically Shaken!

At the end of the service, the church would have prayer teams all over the congregation. They announced that you could have as much prayer as you wanted, so I did. I went throughout the assembly getting prayer. I do not remember how many times their prayer team prayed for me, but it was a lot. I told one of my friends that I came with that I did not feel any different. The lights would then start flickering, signifying that it was time to leave the church.

The service was over, and I was like, oh no, now we must drive home. I did not think I received anything. To be honest, I felt a little disappointed. We started driving home, and I started feeling waves going through my belly, and the closer we got home to Ocala, the waves started getting stronger. My body started to shake uncontrollably, and my friends experienced the same thing. I believe my body could not take all that the Lord had given me, plus I think He was doing a powerful cleansing.

I shook for three days and could not sleep. I remember complaining to the Lord that I had to work at 5 am and there was no way I could handle this, so after three days, the shaking had ceased. I will never forget that time, and I look back at that time with tears asking the Lord to do it again in my life. I am hungrier today than I have ever been. Lord pour out Your Spirit in a more excellent way!

Word Of Faith Church And Meeting My Wife

I had such a desire in my heart to learn more of God's word. When a friend invited me to visit the local Word of Faith Church. I remember sitting there that first-time hearing Pastor Tim Gilligan speak. I was amazed at the teaching of the word. It was like I had eaten a good dinner somewhere. The Lord knew what I needed, and he was setting me up. He would move me there to get more grounded in God's word and, I had a word from the Lord that my wife would be there. I asked the Lord who could she be and trusted Him that I would meet her.

I was always involved with prayer, and I would go with my friends every time there was a prayer meeting on Saturday nights. I remember sitting in the front row, and the presence of God came on me while this amazing-looking blonde girl was praying in tongues. I thought she was beautiful, and I heard the Lord say to me in my Spirit that she was my wife.

I was like, "Wow! We would become friends and shared common interests like prayer and revival," but at first, she did not want anything to do with me. I remember asking her if she would like to go to a Christian play with me the following Wednesday, and she gave me an odd excuse stating that she didn't know what she was doing that day, and she could not plan that far ahead. I thought, Lord, I was asking her to go to this play as a friend. The Lord gave me instructions to leave her alone and pray. After that, she would come up to me and give me a hug when I would see her. I thought, Lord, this is working. I will continue to do what You are telling me to do.

We would then become closer friends traveling together to revivals such as Rodney Howard Browne meetings and the Brownsville Revival meetings in Pensacola. Something started changing! My heart was getting closer to her, and she said later her heart was changing as well. I remember giving her a stuffed cat as a gift and her coming to a prayer meeting at my house where we would kiss for the first time. Later, before Christmas I would ask her to marry me, and we would be married the next year on June 13th, 1998. It was one of the happiest days of my life. All praise goes to King Jesus!

Chapter 6

Pensacola Bound and Ministry Training

The Move To Pensacola, Florida, For Bible School

Within six months of our wedding, Tami and I were on our way to live in Pensacola and be trained for ministry at the Brownsville Revival School of Ministry (BRSM). It was financially hard on us. Our house in Ocala needed to be sold and we lived in a small mobile home in Pensacola. We needed the Lord to come through for us quickly to sell our house in Ocala because we were paying tuition, mortgage in Ocala, and rent on our new trailer.

We came down to our last month where we needed God to come through for us or we would go bankrupt and have the bank foreclose on our house. Tami and I prayed and fasted for three days. After the third day, I received an offer on the house. We took the request, but we received terrible advice from the realtor and ended up having to pay money at the closing. We were still praising God because we were now free from the mortgage payments. The Lord came through for us! Praise God!

Brownsville Revival School Of Ministry

Brownsville Revival School of Ministry was life changing. We had over a thousand students from all over the world. Everyone was so hungry for the Lord, ready to be equipped and be sent out to the nations. I remember walking into the chapel service on the first day, hearing all the people going after Jesus. The tears ran down my face. I knew I was home. The presence of God was amazing!

Chapter 7

The Call to Pray, Evangelize, and Preach

After The Brownsville Revival Days

The day I graduated from bible school, there was a massive split in the Revival and bible school. We had to pray and decide on where we would go from there. Dr. Brown was starting a new school and a church called FIRE (Fellowship for International Revival and Evangelism). My wife still had one semester left to attend, and I was going into my third year which was mostly internship. Tami and I prayed about it together and concluded that our relationships were with the new school's faculty, so we decided to finish our schooling with FIRE.

I had a chance to travel some and go on some mission trips. Tami and I loved to pray, and we got involved with the prayer team at FIRE Church. Sister Carolyn Farias was our prayer leader, and we learned so much from her. She taught us how to be led by the Holy Spirit to pray. I remember the team coming together for prayer on the morning of September 11th, 2001. While we were praying, someone ran into the room shouting that planes had struck the twin towers.

Through Sister Carolyn's leadership, the Holy Spirit would guide us through prayer that morning. We would then come out to watch the television watching the towers in New York City come down. It was a scary moment. Our nation would never be the same.

My Life Changed Direction

I was about to be set up. One day, my wife came home and said to me that she had signed me up for a mentoring class with our third-year internship teacher Brother Bert Farias and told me that I had an appointment with him on a specific date. She handed me a form to fill out, and I was to bring it in at the interview. I will never forget it. One of the questions was what I thought an evangelist was. Immediately I wrote down Luke 4:18.

In the interview Brother Bert looked at me and said he had never had anyone put down Luke 4 as an answer and picked me for the evangelist group. The group went through evangelism mentorship and put everything we learned into practice by going on some trips. I even got to go on some trips with Brother Bert.

Everything I learned from Sister Carolyn and Brother Bert was life changing. Having a prayer life was most important, and the Lord was about to use it in a big way!

Because I Heard You Pray - Kumba, Cameroon 2003

I had the privilege of going on this incredible trip to Cameroon in 2003, and I will never forget it as long as I live. I was a part of a missions' team lead by Brother Bert Farias. The vision was to surround the city of Kumba with ten teams of evangelists and preach at the same time. We would appoint home church leaders to take care of the new converts. It was amazing! We had many souls born again in the three weeks I was there.

I was so encouraged when one of the home church pastors, Pastor Peter, wrote me a letter. Peter was a very humble man, and he wrote me a note about the new converts and how they were doing. I was amazed as I read about how these new converts were growing in their faith. Praise be to the name of Jesus!

Commissioned To Preach

I share this story wherever the Lord sends me because I believe it was the start of my calling to preach. My heart has always been to serve, and I went on this trip to do just that. I wanted to help in whatever capacity the Lord wanted me to. I had no idea what was about to happen as Brother Bert was picking the teams out.

One by one, evangelists were being picked. I remember saying that I would be happy to serve any one of the evangelists chosen. I then heard my name, Rudy Waters! Inside I was full of fear! I had never preached in front of crowds like this before. I had always been content to be an intercessor and pray. Yes, I had done some street evangelism and some brief preaching at the local Salvation Army in Pensacola, but I had never preached in front of a large crowd and let alone in another country. I was like, what would I say? What would I preach? The enemy was trying to intimidate me! It was my time to lead, and I was overwhelmed with fear!

Because I Heard You Pray

I have never forgotten this moment in my life. We had a signifi-cant intercessory prayer time every day, and then we would be sent out to preach all over the city of Kumba, Cameroon. I always love prayer and intercession because of my time praying with seasoned praying warriors. I had two women disciple me in prayer, and one of them was Brother Bert's wife, Sister Carolyn. She trained both my wife and I in prayer. I had no clue that the Lord would use all those years of training by seasoned mentors to prepare me for preaching in the streets. As soon as the prayer time was over, reality set in for me. Soon I would be preaching to the lost in Africa.

The enemy was still attacking me with intense fear. Brother Bert came up to me with one of the most encouraging words that I have ever received in my life. He said to me that he knew I could preach because he had heard me pray. Suddenly the Holy Spirit came all over me! Immediately boldness came over me, and the fear was gone.

I had received the commission to preach, and I knew that all those years of praying had paid off. I had something inside me that the Holy Spirit could use to reach the lost and broken people. It was time to get them, and He was going to fill my mouth with what He wanted me to say, and He did! Acts 4:31 had become a reality! Every time I was about to preach, the Lord had given me something to share. Many souls got saved, healed, and touched by the Lord in those three weeks, and I will never forget it!

Chapter 8

Wilderness Season and Fresh Fire of Revival

A Wilderness Season

I had no idea that the Lord was about to bring me into a wilderness season of my life. Everything seemed to be going well. At least for ministry. We had a fantastic group of people going after lost souls. The leaders at FIRE Church announced that the whole church would be moving to North Carolina. Tami and I prayed, and we felt that we were to stay in Pensacola. We were meeting with an on-fire group at Brother Bert and Carolyn Farias's house.

We all felt led to start a church in Pensacola, and we did for a short season. However, Brother Bert decided that he was not a pastor, so he and Sister Carolyn decided to give the building to another pastor in Pensacola. They would then move away to the New England area. We were again left behind praying. We still felt that we were to stay in Pensacola. The Lord led us to a church called

Kingsway. We served there for around nine years. I didn't realize how much everyone leaving Pensacola affected me, but it did. Also, I had more family responsibilities, so I pretty much gave up on all evangelism ministries. Instead, I served with my wife in the children's church for around nine years and it was a joy.

March 9th, 2014 - The Day That Rudy Waters Died To Himself

What an extraordinary day! I believe the Lord had burned all the desire for ministry and the pulpit out of me. I was finishing up with my last semester of college pursuing a business degree and was content with serving in children's church assisting my wife as she taught the precious three- to five-year-old children we had loved all those years.

I had no desire for pulpit ministry at all. God had burned it all out of me. I believe He knew now I was ready to not take any glory for myself. He was about to change my life forever.

On the evening of March 9th, 2014, one of my mentors had gone to be with the Lord. I had heard him preach probably hun-dreds of times. He was now in the arms of Jesus! I was in my son's room praying, and news came in that Steve Hill, the evangelist of the Brownsville Revival, had died. Suddenly it struck my heart that

I was not doing what the Lord had called me to do. I had no idea that ministers from all over the world were doing the same thing. Ministers were repenting across the globe. I got on my face and cried out in repentance. Screaming, "I am sorry, Lord, for being so distracted when there are souls out there to be reached."

I will never forget His still small voice speaking to me, asking me this question, "Would you be satisfied with my presence and go to the streets to reach the lost?" I said I would, and have not looked back. I got on the cross, died to myself, and the Lord raised me that day. The Holy Spirit has been with me every step of the way.

Praise the Lord for Him giving me another chance! He is the God of many opportunities! I thank the Lord for His mercy!

Mini Revival Breaks Out

I had no idea what was about to happen. That Friday, there was a service at Brownsville Assembly of God to honor Steve's life, and it was wonderful. I heard all the stories about Steve's life, and they continue to light the flame in my heart to reach the lost.

My all-time favorite sermon Steve preached was, "You Can't Have It". It was about the crown that Jesus would give us to throw at His feet. At the funeral, they showed some video clippings from this sermon in the ceremony. While I watched the video of Steve preaching this sermon, the burden of God to reach lost souls was restored in my life.

The Sunday after the ceremony, our pastor got up to speak from the pulpit at King's Way Church. He asked someone to share a picture. I believe he was about to share a photo that many of us had seen a day earlier. It turned out that somebody had taken a picture of Jeri, the wife of Steve Hill, during the ceremony.

A large angel formed in the image behind her, and our pastor was about to show it. Suddenly he was taken by a vision of the Lord that he continues to share to this day.

The church's atmosphere shifted, and the glory of the Lord came into the building. It was hard to stand up. Our pastor fell to the floor and stayed there for many hours. We waited and pressed into the Lord for hours as our pastor was on the floor, and he would later share the vision of Jesus walking into the room.

Jesus walked right up to him, holding a banner in one hand, and in the other, Jesus washed Him with the fire of God. We were all changed, and revival broke out.

Miracles Break Out!

I remember this like this was yesterday. I was at an evangelism event at Brownsville Assembly on one of the days we did not meet at revival, and I met this amazing mom and a young man with Down Syndrome. I was amazed at his pure heart and hunger for the Lord, so I invited them to come to the revival.

The young man came, and he worshipped the Lord with so much purity. He kept going to Pastor Rick, tugging on his leg to tell him something during worship. Pastor Rick got the microphone and had this young man share what was on his heart. The boy kept saying, "He is here." Pastor asked him, "Where?" and the boy pointed to the back of the room.

It turned out that was the exact location where the pastor first saw the vision of Jesus. The leaders then prayed for the young man's feet, and God healed him. They then called for the sick, and I witnessed probably one of the greatest miracles so far in my life. There was a blind lady that had no color in her eyes, and God instantly healed her. We all witnessed the miracle of the color in her eyes coming back.

After that, suddenly, people were receiving healings from the Lord all over the building. The revival had catapulted forward.

Meetings went to a tent and then from various cities in the Gulf Coast region. The revival lasted around eight months.

Chapter 9

Walking into God's Calling of Evangelism

The Start Of Evangelizing

During that revival, I started serving on evangelism teams. We would go out to reach the lost a couple of hours before the church services. This one testimony stands out to me. Richard Davis and I had reconnected back from our BRSM/FIRE School days. He drove down from Tuscaloosa to help. Ned, Richard, and I were on a team, and we walked by a lady on her bike. She immediately fell off her bike and started manifesting demons.

We prayed for her, and she got back on her bicycle to drive off. Suddenly, she fell out again. The owner of one of the stores came out a couple of times, warning us. He had no idea what was going on and threatened to call the police. We got her back up, and she brought us to a couple of her friends, so we had a chance to witness to them.

Brother Richard had a word of knowledge for one of the guys, and the other gentleman had a problem with his neck. As Ned prayed for him, I heard the man's neck crack, and the man yelled out that we healed his blanking neck. Ned told him that Jesus did it. These folks met the Lord that day for sure, and I believe they were never the same.

Bold Acts

I will never forget what the Lord said to me a few years ago. He said, "The antidote for fear of man is for you to pray for boldness." Immediately, I went to Acts 4:29-31 *"Now, Lord, look on their threats, and grant to Your servants that with all boldness they may speak Your word, by stretching out Your hand to heal, and that signs and wonders may be done through the name of Your holy Servant Jesus And when they had prayed, the place where they were assembled together was shaken; and they were all filled with the Holy Spirit, and they spoke the word of God with boldness."*

The disciples were facing all kinds of fear and intimidation, even death. They knew the key was to pray for boldness to continue the Lord's work.

After returning to the Lord on March 9th, 2014, I followed my friend Joel Crumpton on Facebook. I saw all the testimonies of healings that were happening, and it sparked my curiosity, so I contacted him and planned a trip to Atlanta, Georgia.

Joel had received some revelation from the Lord on declaring. I loved it, and I use it, but I will never forget one of the things he shared with me on boldness, which he put in his book, *You Can Do the Works of Jesus: From Theory to Reality*. Joel said, *"Boldness is faith acted out. It is courage in the midst of fear; it is daring to speak and act even though you feel intimidated. Boldness is a necessary ingredient of faith. Fear and intimidation will always be present when an opportunity to minister healing to someone in public comes up. Don't allow those feelings to cause you to shrink back in unbelief. Deny yourself and do what Jesus would do."*

In Atlanta, I got to put what I learned from Joel into action by taking evangelism to the streets. I had no idea what I was about to witness. My life was going to be changed forever. Miracles took place, and the power of God changed people's lives.

Here's one of the miracles that I witnessed. The miracle happened right after we fed the homeless. Joel walked up to a girl; she was in a walking boot and had to use crutches to walk. She was with a team visiting from Cincinnati, Ohio. Joel asked her what happened to her, and the girl next to her told him that she broke her foot, was in a lot of pain and could not put any weight on it. Joel said to her that he had good news for her. The Kingdom of Heaven had come near to her today.

He said that if she would give him her hand that the power of God would flow through her and heal her right now. She did, and Joel spoke in the Name of Jesus Christ be healed right now. He told her to check herself and see if she could put any weight on her foot. Her countenance changed! All the pain had left, and she was speechless! She started putting weight on her foot and walked with no pain. The Lord instantly healed her. All her friends from Cincinnati were amazed, and they joked about having to buy her new sneakers because she had only brought one shoe. We all gave glory to Jesus! Our Lord is amazing!

I went back home from that trip, totally fired up to believe the Lord for miracles, and I had no idea that the Lord was going to work so quickly, but something had changed in my life. The Lord had given me boldness, and I was willing to step out in faith. I could not wait to pray for people back in Pensacola. Miracles were about to happen.

I was allowed to serve on the Salvation Army's prayer team for local outreach. They broke us up into groups of two to pray for people, and I got a chance to serve with a local pastor. We had an opportunity to pray for a man who had eight surgeries on his hip, and he was in a lot of pain.

I told him that I had good news for him and that the Kingdom of Heaven had come near him today. I said if he would give me his hand, the power of God would heal him. Then I said, "In the name of Jesus Christ of Nazareth, be healed right now."

We confessed more healing scriptures over the man. He could not believe it, but he had significantly less pain. We declared healing again and thanked the Lord for his healing. I took the man's crutches and had him take a step of faith. The man was shocked the pain had left his body, and he was able to walk around without crutches. We talked to him about giving his life to the Lord one hundred percent, and he rededicated his life to Him. The Lord gets all the glory!

That miracle changed my life forever! Friends, the enemy was coming at me with all kinds of fear and intimidation. All sorts of thoughts and questions entered my mind.

I heard the enemy say, "You are going to look like a fool. What if nothing happens and he is not healed?" I decided to go for it and be willing to look like a fool for Jesus. I dared to believe His word and look what happened. The Lord came, healed this precious person's body, and a soul came to the Lord. You can do it too, my friend. You have the same Holy Spirit living in you that Jesus had. Pray for boldness daily and step out in faith and watch fear bow to the name of Jesus! I believe the Lord will be with you every step of the way. Get ready for miracles to happen!

Kingdom Of Heaven Revelation

I was amazed at this miracle. In my quiet time with the Lord, He gave me some revelation. He said, "This is why you declare, 'The Kingdom of Heaven has come near you." When you claim the Kingdom of Heaven, you are proclaiming the Kingdom of Heaven coming to earth as it is in Heaven.

There is no sickness and disease in Heaven; therefore, by proclaiming the Kingdom of Heaven over people who are sick, you are declaring the Kingdom of Heaven over that sickness and disease. Sickness and disease must flee because the Kingdom of Heaven is proclaimed."

Matthew 6:10 says, *"Your kingdom come; your will be done on earth as it is in heaven."*

We are carriers of the Kingdom of Heaven everywhere we go. Where we go, the atmosphere should change to the Kingdom of Heaven. We are the temple of the Holy Ghost. The mystery is Christ in us, the hope of glory. Go and change the atmosphere of the earth and the atmosphere of people's circumstances in God's power, which is in Jesus' Name.

More Of The Love Of Jesus In My Heart

Before I go any further to talk about methods of evangelism that I have learned, I must share what happened to me through a transition time. I was transitioning from Kingsway Church, and I started visiting a church called Freedom Church on Sunday evenings. There was something different when I walked in. I needed some time to soak in the Lord. Freedom Church, through worship, was taking us into the presence of the Lord. I hadn't experienced that in a long time. It was a fresh breath of air for me, and after testify-ing to my family, they started coming.

Something was different about the leadership there. I would of-ten shake hands in church, but these guys would come up and hug me. One pastor would hug me until I gave him a big hug back. Af-ter several months, I started having a heart change. I wanted to do the same. I just loved everybody. The Lord had transformed my heart.

You see, I learned that the more we get into the presence of God, the more we become like Him. The Lord gave me a revelation some time ago about the fruit of the Spirit in Galatians 5:22-23 TLB *"But when the Holy Spirit controls our lives, he will produce this kind of fruit in us: love, joy, peace, patience, kindness, goodness, faithfulness, gentleness, and self-control; and here there is no con-flict with Jewish laws".*

You see, what was happening to me was the more I spent time with the Lord, the more of the fruit of the Holy Spirit was bub-bling out of my life. The Lord was healing me of all wounds and re-placing it with His fruit, and it was manifesting to everyone I met.

We can use the many different methods that we learn to reach the lost, but the Lord must be in it.

I love the quote from Leonard Ravenhill when asked about evangelism methods. He said, "All evangelism methods are good as long as God is in it." I love that.

We can learn methods and they are a great tool for us to pull out of our Batman belt, but I love to use them when the Holy Spirit shows me while I'm ministering to people. The Lord gave me this vision for our Freedom in Action Team at Church, "We have fallen so in love with Him (God) that we have gotten a hold of His heart's desire - that no one should perish - and we are compelled to tell everyone about Him and His love for them.

The only thing you need to join this team is to just be yourself, so filled up with His presence that everyone you love and pray for encounters the glory of God. Our mission is to share the good news of the gospel, pray for the sick and see them healed, raise the dead, and baptize people in the Holy Spirit." That is what it's all about. Being so filled up with Him that His presence goes with us wherever we go.

As my mentor Joel Crumpton would always say, "We just become the person who delivers the package." So, come on the journey with me as I teach you some methods of evangelism that I have learned, and Holy Spirit will bring them out of you when you need them. I am so excited for you! It is going to be a wonderful journey, and I pray that the Lord will give you a heart for the lost and broken-hearted.

Chapter 10

Methods of

Evangelism and Testimonies

Try Tears - Compassion

This is my favorite method, so I will start here. I have never forgotten this quote by Charles Spurgeon, "Winners for souls must first be weepers for souls". I have learned this through trial and error that the more time we spend in prayer with the Lord, the more we get His heart, which is for the lost. Jesus's heart is that no one should perish, and souls are going into eternity every second. Many of us want to pray for a couple of minutes and then hit the streets to share the gospel. That is like going out to chop down a tree with a dull ax. The tree would get chopped down, but it would take a lot longer. The work would go much quicker with a sharp ax.

I love this story that I heard from back in the early days of the Salvation Army. Some of William Booth's leaders wrote him a letter. They were distraught because they did not see a lot of fruit in the ministry. General Booth would report back to them to "Try tears."

These leaders took his advice, and they saw the Lord move powerfully. I will never forget the times I saw Evangelist Steve Hill preach at the Brownsville Revival. You could tell he spent time with the Lord weeping for the lost. When he would come out to preach, you could see the tears running down his face. Steve would preach a powerful message against sin and declare that folks come to repent at the altars if they had sin in their lives.

No matter how hard the message was, we knew that Steve had been with the Lord and cared about us because of the compassion he had for the people's lives. He got it from spending time with the Lord. The anointing was strong, and people would run to the altar by the thousands. This is what we need in America again. Believers should go into the secret place and weep again for the state of our country, the world, and lost souls. When we come out of the prayer closet, we come out with the compassion the Lord has for the lost.

Here is the method I learned. When we go out to pray for someone, we look them in the eyes with heartfelt compassion and ask them to tell us the truth. We ask them if they know Jesus, not if they know about Him. As Steve Hill would say, "religion is hanging around the cross, but Christianity is getting on the cross." Many people, especially in the US, want a "Get Out of Hell Free Card "and want to live for themselves. What the Lord wants is total surrender to Jesus! He wants us to get on the cross, die to ourselves, and then He raises us and sends us out to the world. Praise God that is the answer!

Don't Be Like A Pharisee, Be Like The Tax Collector

I had the opportunity to go on Bourbon Street in New Orleans with a team of on-fire students from the School of Urban Missions and some awesome friends from Rusk, Texas. This was one of the most challenging mission trips I have ever taken in my life. I was overwhelmed with the pride of the people. The folks were flaunting every sin I could imagine. I could not believe that they would even involve minor children in their revelry.

I usually would do evangelism where everyone would receive prayer, but these people did not want me anywhere near them. They wanted to sin freely, and I felt grieved in my heart for them. I suddenly realized that the Lord was taking me through a season of experiencing what we read about in scripture. I thought about what Noah must have felt like when he preached for a hundred years, and not one person would listen to him. The Lord reminded me of what Lot must have felt like in Sodom and Gomorrah, and I was reminded about the revelry of the children of Israel when they built the Golden Calf in the book of Exodus.

The Lord was breaking me, and he was birthing prayer and intercession in me. Jesus reminded of the Apostle Paul, who became like all men to all people, so that some would come to the Lord, and that is what we did throughout the two days we were there. The Lord led us to people so He could snatch them out of destruction. God is faithful, and He did!

Don't Be Like A Pharisee

Luke 18:9-14 says, *"Also He spoke this parable to some who trusted in themselves that they were righteous and despised others: "Two men went up to the temple to pray, one a Pharisee and the other a tax collector. The Pharisee stood and prayed thus with himself, 'God, I thank You that I am not like other men—extortioners, unjust, adulterers, or even this tax collector. I fast twice a week; I give tithes of all that I possess."*

Many things grieved me throughout Mardi Gras, but what bothered me the most was when I heard my brothers and sisters in Christ preaching to the people saying that God hated them.

I immediately stopped to pray for my brothers and sisters. The Lord showed me that he hated sin but loved these precious people. I heard many times about the words of Jesus when He said, "*Father forgive them for they do not know what they do,*" and Stephen said, "*Father do not hold this sin against them.*" Yes, if these folks were to die in their sin, the Lord would say, "*depart from me; I never knew you,*" but today is the day of salvation, and He does not want anyone to perish.

I prayed for our brothers and sisters to preach with compassion and tears. I thought about Charles Spurgeon's words that said, "He that is a winner of souls, must first be a weeper of souls." May we not become like a Pharisee that says, "*Father, I am glad I am not like these sinners,*" but may we see with the Father's eyes and let Him break us for these precious people. Yes, we may have a stern message, but let these people see the tears in our eyes and the compassion that we have for them!

I remember Steve Hill, who I saw preach over hundreds of times. Steve would always have a message of repentance and holiness, but I knew he cared. He would still have tears in his eyes, and I knew he cared about the very souls of the people. May we let the Lord break us for the lost, so when we preach to lost people, they will know that we care about them, and the Love of God will bring them to repentance!

He Thought God Hated Him

The Lord did something extraordinary in the life of Jonathan right there on Bourbon Street. Brother Levi Lutz had me pray for a couple of homeless people, and I turned around and saw Levi praying for Jonathan. It turned out that Jonathan told Levi not to look at him that way and grabbed him. Levi said enough is enough and started preaching the gospel to Jonathan, holding on to him. Levi told him that he needed to get right with God and that the Lord loved him.

I immediately came over to help Levi pray for him, and Jonathan kept screaming out that God hated him and how the Lord did not love him. Levi continued to tell Jonathan that the Lord loved him, and he needed to give his life to Him. After fighting in prayer, Levi convinced Jonathan to pray a prayer of salvation in his own words. We then continued to pray for him to receive deliverance because Jonathan continued to say the Lord did not love him and started to manifest demons. We immediately cast them out, and Jonathan told us that we messed his life up (in a good way). He said that he was married and needed to get back to his wife, but he continued coming back to hug us and kept telling us how we messed his life up. God is amazing, and what a powerful testimony, and I believe that Jonathan will never be the same!

Let's Be Like The Tax Collector

Luke 18:13-14 says, *"And the tax collector, standing afar off, would not so much as raise his eyes to heaven, but beat his breast, saying, 'God, be merciful to me a sinner!' I tell you; this man went down to his house justified rather than the other; for everyone who exalts himself will be humbled, and he who humbles himself will be exalted."*

I believe there were a lot of Jonathan's out there that night. The preaching was mostly fire and brimstone. It was mainly out of self-righteous indignation. I did not hear much compassion for the lost people in their voices. May we remember that we used to be like them at one time and remember what the Lord has brought us out of. May we see the people how God sees them and pray for the

Lord to forgive them for they know not what they do. May we pray for the Lord to open their eyes and let them see Him! May we show these folks how much we care about them and how much the Lord wants them to come home. Yes, we can preach repentance, holiness, and truth, but let us do it out of compassion, tears, and love!

The Power Of A Testimony

I believe the most powerful thing we can do is share our testimony with someone we witness to about the Lord. I love the saying that a person with a testimony is never at the mercy of someone with an opinion. It is your testimony of what the Lord did in your life. Most people listen when you tell them how the Lord changed you. I have so many stories of people touched by the Lord after I shared my testimony and prayed for them. It is one of my favorite ways to share the gospel.

Your Testimony Increases Faith

When we share our testimony with someone, it causes the testimony's hearer to have faith to believe that God will do a miracle for them. God's miracle-working power is in the stories of the Bible. Confidence rises in the believer's belief that God can work a miracle for them when we read God's word. Here are some examples.

Jesus Was Our Example In John 1:32

The Holy Spirit descended on Jesus and remained on Him with the Father's voice testifying, saying, this is my beloved son in whom I am well pleased.

The Woman With The Issue Of Blood In Mark 5

The woman used every resource she had on doctors. I am sure she heard the testimonies of Jesus and set out saying that if I only may touch his clothes. Fighting through the crowd, she felt Jesus's clothes and the power went out of him, and the blood was dried up. Instantly, God healed her. Jesus has power, but this precious woman acted on the testimonies that she heard and activated her faith. Jesus even told her that her faith made her well. Her testimony sparked a revival.

Gennesaret In Mark 6

I love this! Jesus and His disciples came to Gennesaret and anchored there. Immediately they were recognized by the people. Testimony had gotten out of Jesus's healing power. The people immediately started bringing the sick to him so that He may heal them. My favorite part was when they entered the villages, cities, and country; the people would immediately beg Jesus that they may touch the hem of His garment so they would be made well. How in the world would they know about this had they not heard of the precious woman healed earlier? I believe the testimony had gotten out to Gennesaret, sparking faith in the people. Revival had broken out in Gennesaret. God's power was changing people! Praise the Lord!

How About The Disciples Receiving The Holy Spirit?

As soon as the disciples got the Holy Spirit, they shared everything on what they had seen and heard. A disabled beggar received a miracle when Peter and John prayed for him. The religious leaders warned them not to speak about Jesus, but they could not disprove that a miracle had taken place. Most of all, they marveled that Peter and John were uneducated and unlearned men realizing that they had been with Jesus. God's miracle power was flowing through them. I believe the testimony of what happened with the disabled beggar sparked a revival because later, thousands of people came into the church. Praise God!

Brownsville Revival - The Ward Sisters

I shared earlier that my Sunday school teacher shared a video with me of these two teenage girls, who the Lord touched at the Brownsville Revival. One sister would share how she was on the floor reaching up, the Lord would grab her hand, almost lifting her off the ground. I was amazed when she shared. The Lord told her to not let go of Him or she would fall.

While sharing her testimony, the other sister would be shaking uncontrollably. She then gets overcome by the Lord, saying there is not much more time. God wants everybody to come to Him. The Lord's presence would hit their church, sending the congregation into a time of intercession for the lost. Believers were falling onto the floor, groaning with travail for the lost. I remember feeling the presence of the Lord while watching them and saying I must get to that church.

The Ward sister's testimonies went around the world, sparking a hunger in people to come to Pensacola, Florida to meet with the Lord. Hundreds of thousands of souls would be born again at the Brownsville Revival. As the people came, the Lord would set them ablaze with the fires of revival, sparking a hunger in them to spread the revival worldwide. Many believers came to Brownsville to be equipped for ministry and they are now serving God on the mission field today. Yes, a testimony is powerful, and may the Lord do it again, in a greater way!

Baptism Of The Holy Spirit

One of the most amazing things I have learned in street ministry is that we do not have to wait to pray for folks to receive the Holy Spirit's baptism. Reading the book of Acts, people received the Holy Spirit before or after being baptized in water, which means to me that believers do not have to wait to receive. It's a free gift that God has given us. All we have to do is ask and we will receive. I have learned from two amazing mentors how to teach believers how to receive this gift.

I tend to use Evangelist Warren Galvin's method a little more because he would talk about the Holy Spirit's baptism sometimes even before preaching salvation. Warren would get a person interested in receiving God's power to live a Christian life, and then he would talk to them about making sure they were right with God first before praying for them to receive Holy Spirit.

A high percentage of the people would give their hearts to the then they would pray to receive the gift. Most people would have unforgettable encounters with the Lord and it's always glorious.

Others would receive Holy Spirit not feeling anything, which is okay because we do not walk by feelings; we walk by faith. Here's the teachings I put together from what I learned from both methods.

1. John's Baptism Was A Baptism Of Repentance.

Acts 19:1-7 says, *"While Apollos was at Corinth, Paul took the road through the interior and arrived at Ephesus. And finding some disciples and asked them, "Did you receive the Holy Spirit when you believed? "They answered, "No, we have not even heard that there is a Holy Spirit."*

So Paul asked, "Then what baptism did you receive?" "John's baptism," they replied. Paul said, "John's baptism was a baptism of repentance. He told the people to believe in the one coming after him, that is, in Jesus." On hearing this, they were baptized in the name of the Lord Jesus. When Paul placed his hands on them, the Holy Spirit came on them, and they spoke in tongues and prophesied. There were about twelve men in all."

2. Jesus Commanded The Disciples To Wait And Receive Holy Spirit.

John 7:37-39 says, *"On the last day, that great day of the feast, Jesus stood and cried out, saying, "If anyone thirsts, let him come to Me and drink. He who believes in Me, as the Scripture has said, out of his heart will flow rivers of living water." But this He spoke concerning the Spirit, whom those believing in Him would receive; for the Holy Spirit was not yet given, because Jesus was not yet glorified."*

Luke 24:49 says, *"Behold, I send the Promise of My Father upon you; but tarry in the city of Jerusalem until you are endued with power from on high."*

Acts 1:4, 5 says, *"And being assembled together with them, He commanded them not to depart from Jerusalem, but to wait for the Promise of the Father, "which," He said, "you have heard from Me; for John truly baptized with water, but you shall be baptized with the Holy Spirit not many days from now."* It is not an option, or suggestion for believers; it was a commandment by Jesus Himself!

3. When We Get Born Again, The Holy Spirit Dwells In Us.

John 14:17 says, *"...the Spirit of truth, whom the world cannot receive, because it neither sees Him nor knows Him; but you know Him, for He dwells with you and will be in you."*

We receive a measure of the Holy Spirit when we become born again. I always share with people its like having a well inside our bellies waiting to be turned into a river of living water.

4. Wihen The Baptism Of The Holy Spirit Comes On Us, We Receive Power.

Acts 1:8 says, *"But you shall receive power when the Holy Spirit has come upon you; and you shall be witnesses to Me in Jerusalem, and in all Judea and Samaria, and to the end of the earth."*

5. Reasons To Be Baptized In The Holy Spirit.

A. Acts 1:4,5 - He commands us to.

B. Acts 1:8 - We receive power.

C. Acts 10:46 - We praise the Lord.

D. 1 Cor. 14:4 - We edify ourselves.

E. Acts 2:11 - We declare the wonders of God.

F. Acts 10:46 - We speak directly to God.

G. Romans 8:26,27 - We pray for the perfect will of God.

H. Jude 20 - We build up our most holy faith.

6. We Ask And Then We Receive The Holy Spirit Just Like We Receive A Gift.

Luke 11:11-13 says, *"If a son asks for bread from any father among you, will he give him a stone? Or if he asks for a fish, will he give him a serpent instead of a fish? Or if he asks for an egg, will he offer him a scorpion? If you then, being evil, know how to give good gifts to your children, how much more will your heavenly Father give the Holy Spirit to those who ask Him!"*

7. We Just Simply Out Of Faith, Speak And The Holy Spirit Will Inspire Us!

Acts 2:4 TPT says, *"They were all filled and equipped with the Holy Spirit and were inspired to speak in tongues-empowered by the Spirit to speak in languages they never learned!"*

The Holy Spirit gave the disciples the power to speak, and we do the same. What a glorious gift He is to the body of Christ! Here's a couple of testimonies of precious people receiving the Holy Spirit's baptism from the harvest field.

Reimagine Event In Pensacola

Susan Carr brought Amanda to the Reimagine Event. She just moved to Pensacola. I asked her if she received the baptism in the Holy Ghost! She said yes, but she was talking about water baptism. I spoke to her about receiving the Holy Ghost's power, and she immediately said she wanted the gift! We prayed for her, and she received the Holy Ghost, fire, and prayed in other tongues! She told us heat was all over her! Praise Jesus!

Jake And The Homeless Mission

My wife and I had several food bags leftover from an outreach, and we were praying on where to go to give them away. Immediately Tami said, "Do you think there is a mission nearby? I looked it up in my map's app, and there was one less than a mile away, so we decided to stop by. I rang the bell, and Jake answered the door. He took all our food bags for the folks at the mission and let us pray for him. We started going back to the car, and a lady called out. She was a lady we prayed for the night before, so we prayed for her again, and while we were praying, Jake came out. He said that the Lord touched him while we prayed for him and that he was so hungry for more of God. We talked to him about receiving the Holy Ghost's power and his prayer language. He was hungry to receive, so we prayed for him. He immediately received Him! The Lord powerfully touched him right there. We are still in communication with Jake. God has a massive plan for him. Praise the Lord!

God's Treasure

The Lord would give me this revelation while praying for a girl at the International House of Pancakes. She was a waitress and started telling us all her hardships in life. In prayer, the Lord had me tell her that she was God's beautiful jewel. I started telling her the parable Jesus gave us about the man and a field. Here is the scripture context. Matthew 13:44 says, *"Again, the kingdom of heaven is like treasure hidden in a field, which a man found and hid; and for joy, over it, he goes and sells all that he has and buys that field."*

With the compassion of the Lord in my heart and tears flowing from my eyes the Lord started giving me words to say to her from this scripture. I told her that she was the treasure in the field, God's jewel. The Lord said that she was precious, beautiful to Him and that the Lord had sold everything He had to repurchase her. God used His best by sending His Son to die for her. He died in her place; to pay for her sin. He bought the precious treasure in the field, which was her. The girl was so overwhelmed that she ran off in tears of conviction, but I knew the Lord had started healing her broken heart. I was honored to be there at the right time for this precious girl. She told us what she was going through. It gripped my heart, and I could feel the weight of it. The cares of this life weighed her down. The Lord sent me at the right time to encourage her through this challenging time. The Lord is good! I only use this method when the Holy Spirit leads me to share it, but it is powerful when He does. We are His treasure. The Lord paid the price, the ultimate price to repurchase us. Praise the Lord that He did.

ABC's Of Salvation

By far, one of the easiest evangelism methods that I have learned to share the gospel. Here are the method's scriptural foundations, and you can memorize them very quickly.

- Romans 3:23 - *"For <u>all have sinned</u> and fallen short of the glory of God."*

- Acts 16:31 - <u>Believe in Jesus</u> - *"So they said, "Believe on the Lord Jesus Christ, and you will be saved, you and your household."*

- Romans 10:9-10 - <u>Confess with our mouth</u> - *"That if you confess with your mouth the Lord Jesus and believe in your heart that God has raised Him from the dead, you will be saved. For with the heart one believes unto righteousness, and with the mouth confession is made unto salvation."*

Usually, this easy method will come out when I encounter folks daily. All of us have fallen short of God's glory. We are all guilty and will stand before the Father and give an account of our lives. None of our friends will be standing there with us. We will be alone.

Then I share with them about believing. To believe in Jesus, we must decide to turn away from sin and accept what Jesus paid for, which is a price that we cannot pay ourselves. Jesus paid the penalty with His own blood. We must repent of our selfishness and turn to Jesus. He is the only one that paid the cost for our sin.

I remember having a vision one day of a courtroom, and I was standing before the judge. I had the enemy, the devil hurling accusations. He was telling the judge everything that I had done. The judge had the hammer in his hand, and he was about to pronounce me guilty, but someone walked into the room. It was Jesus!

He called out to the judge and spoke. "I paid his fine"! Suddenly sin and shame lifted off me. It was gone. The judge looked at me and said I am giving you a choice. Which one do you choose today? I chose Jesus and got to walk away free!

Lastly, we open our mouths and confess. Declaring is powerful! We are confessing Jesus through our mouths, then we leave the life of sin and give our lives to Jesus. Out of the mouth, we are acknowledging our sin, asking Him to forgive us, believing what He did for us, declaring our salvation, and surrendering our very lives to Him.

When we do this with a pure heart, old things pass away, and all things become new—no more looking back. From that time on, we are new creatures in the Lord through prayer and His word. Praise God!

The Roman Road

The Roman Road is like the ABCs of Salvation. They call it the Roman Road because most of the scriptures are from the book of Romans. You can take these scriptures and walk people through each scripture, leading them to a revelation of salvation through Jesus. It is an easy method, and I love it. Here it is.

Sin - Romans 3:23

"For all have sinned and fall short of the glory of God. Because of sin, we all died. Death entered the world because of Adam and Eve's disobedience to God."

Death - Romans 6:23

"For the wages of sin is death, but the gift of God is eternal life in Christ Jesus." I will usually tell them God had a plan through the seed of a woman promised in Genesis to restore the relationship to Him.

Love - Romans 5:8

"But God demonstrated His love toward us, in that while we were yet sinners, Christ died for us." The Lord sent his very own son to die on the cross to pay for my sin and yours.

Faith - Ephesians 2:8-9

"For by grace you have been saved through faith, and that not of yourselves, it is the gift of God; not as of works, so that no one may boast." We come to Jesus by faith. Faith means trust. We are trusting what Jesus did for us. We cannot work our way into heaven. It is a gift. We repent by turning away from a selfish life and surrender everything by receiving Jesus's gift of salvation.

Life - Romans 10:9-10

"If you confess with your mouth Jesus as Lord and believe in your heart that God raised Him from the dead, you will be saved; for with the heart a person believes, resulting in righteousness, and with the mouth he confesses, resulting in salvation." You see, when we do this, there is a heart change. We become a new person. Jesus pulls us from death to life. I remember praying and receiving the Lord. When I opened my eyes, I felt new. Sin lifted off me, and I could see clearly.

I went from listening to Ozzy Osbourne to craving the Lord's music to lift my spirit. I went from drinking massive amounts of alcohol to wanting God's presence in my life. I did not want the things of the world anymore. I surrounded myself with people who could help me grow in the Lord. I honestly was born again!

Repentance From Selfishness

I learned this method from my mentor Evangelist Joel Crumpton, and I use it a lot.

Matthew 3:10 says, *"And even now the axe is laid to the root of the trees. Therefore, every tree which does not bear good fruit is cut down and thrown into the fire."*

If a tree produces bad fruit, the problem is not the fruit, my friend, the problem is with the root system. A bad tree can only produce bad fruit. We cannot expect us to have good fruit if the root system in our lives is terrible. We will continue to make bad fruit. Just taking the bad fruit off the tree and throwing it away does not produce good fruit; bad fruit will grow in its place.

John the Baptist talked about Jesus coming and dealing with the root system of sin. The only way to deal with the sin is through repentance and giving our life to Jesus one hundred percent. We repent, turn to Jesus, and let the Lord burn out every desire of sin in our life. Jesus changes our root system. Through our relationship with the Lord, we then start producing His fruit.

Galatians 5:22-23 TLB says, *"But when the Holy Spirit controls our lives, He will produce this kind of fruit in us: love, joy, peace, patience, kindness, goodness, faithfulness, gentleness, and self-control; and here there is no conflict with Jewish laws."*

We get so filled up with the presence of the Lord; His fruit bubbles out of us to reach the lost world. There is no other way to live! It is exciting!

Different Types Of Soil

This one I learned through many years of evangelizing. When we go out to reach lost souls, I realized that people's hearts are like different soil types. Jesus taught us a parable on the soil of people's hearts in Mark 4:13-20 *"And He said to them, 'Do you not understand this parable? How then will you understand all the parables? The sower sows the word. And these are the ones by the wayside where the word is sown. When they hear, Satan comes immediately and takes away the word that was sown in their hearts. These likewise are the ones sown on stony ground who, when they hear the word, immediately receive it with gladness; and they have no root in themselves, and so endure only for a time. Afterward, when tribulation or persecution arises for the word's sake, immediately they stumble. Now these are the ones sown among thorns; they are the ones who hear the word, and the cares of this world, the deceitfulness of riches, and the desires for other things entering in choke the word, and it becomes unfruitful. But these are the ones sown on good ground, those who hear the word, accept it, and bear fruit: some thirtyfold, some sixty, and some a hundred.'"*

I use this parable a lot when ministering to folks on the streets. Some folks will not receive me at all. They have hard hearts, and I usually will sow a seed by blessing them. Sometimes I bless them and walk away. The enemy could be sending them as a distraction to try and stop me from a divine appointment. I have learned to move on and go to the next person. We must remember that we are sowers and waterers. The Lord is the one that does the work. We are just obeying his word. Then, while we follow His Word, we receive thirty, sixty, and hundred-fold increases in the harvest field. God gets all the glory!

Divine Appointments

I love these, and they do not happen all the time, but I believe the Lord wants us to pray for them. You see, we can be frustrated when these do not always occur. When I was younger, I would be frustrated when I did not see everyone come to the Lord. It's done not in our strength anyway. I love the scripture in 1Cor.3:6-8 that says, *"I planted, Apollos watered, but God gave the increase. So then, neither he who plants is anything, nor he who waters, but God who gives the increase. Now he who plants and he who waters are one, and each one will receive his reward according to his labor."*

I got this revelation from going to a Christ for all Nations Evangelism training. The light went off in my spirit, and all this weight came off me. If we see ourselves as planters and waterers, the pressure comes off us and goes onto the Lord. We do our part, and the Lord does His part. We need to make it simple, spending time with the Lord and having him lead us.

I would pray this a lot in my prayer time. Lord, please give me divine appointments today. I had seen examples of it happening in scripture with Jesus, Paul, Phillip, and others, but I didn't have an exact scripture until I had a brother encourage me to pray a specific scripture. This scripture radically changed the way I prayed, and I will share it with you.

In Colossians 4:3, the scripture says, *"Meanwhile praying also for us, that God would open to us a door for the word, to speak the mystery of Christ, for which I am also in chains,"*

Once I got this revelation, I was like wow! I was praying this way already, and the Lord would bring me these amazing divine appointments. I started expecting them. The Lord would confirm His word with signs following. Here's a couple of our divine appointment testimonies!

Testimony In Tuscaloosa, AL

Pastor Abraham Javine and I pulled up into his driveway after church, and Steven was there asking for work. He was there at the right time. Pastor Javine asked me to pray for him. I prayed for him, and the Lord started filling my mouth with words to say to him. The next thing we knew, Steven was crying, and we were leading him to Jesus! We prayed for him to be free from alcohol, as well. Thank You, Jesus! I know Angels are rejoicing right now!

Fred

Wow, the Lord gave me an incredible divine assignment! Right after the School of Evangelism, I craved Indian Food. I pulled up in front of an Indian Restaurant, but it was only vegetarian. I decided to go to another one down the street, but that one was vegetarian, as well. I decided to stay and eat there anyway.

Fred walked in and sat at a table next to me and ordered what I had! He struck up a conversation with me. I felt like I was doing a radio interview. He interviewed me for over an hour, and I got to preach the gospel to this man, and he came back to the Lord! He said that he was going back to his church that he had not gone to in over a year! I left him with my testimony tract, and he said my testimony was like his situation! Please pray for my friend Fred!

Amazing Testimony

Our team had a huge divine appointment in Northport, Alabama, while traveling to Emma Cameron's house. Pastor Abraham Javine wanted to go to Wal-Mart to get gasoline. When we arrived, I asked if there was a bathroom, and I heard a man named Jimmy talking to the clerk about how he worked all day and was in pain. I asked to pray for him, and he told me he had no feeling in his foot!

Our team lead him to Jesus. Team member Dennis Godwin went to pray for Jimmy's foot, but God healed Jimmy before Dennis even touched him. Jimmy screamed out, "Wait a minute, my foot is tingling, and I feel heat going through my foot! I'm healed, I'm healed!" Jimmy was amazed and gave glory to Jesus! Other people at the gas pumps stopped pumping their gas and just stared. We got kicked out of the gas station by the manager because of the commotion, but praise the Lord, Jimmy got healed that day! Jesus, YOU are amazing!

An Easy One

The Lord loves to give us easy ones while we are obeying Him. While we are sowing and watering, He loves to encourage us by what I call "divine appointments." I have had many of them since serving the Lord, and every time it happens, I am inspired. I pray for them, and I expect them to happen. Usually, when I am out throughout the day doing things like shopping or getting gas, I expect the Lord to set me up. I remember pumping my gas, and a lady called me over to her car and asked me if I would pump her gas for her. I knew it.

The Lord had set me up, and I knew the Lord would have me pray for her. She needed healing in her back. I prayed for her, and the pain left her body. Then I shared the gospel, and she recommitted her life to Jesus. We should expect divine appointments all the time. There are no coincidences throughout the day when people start chatting with us. If we miss it, the Lord is always faithful to give us another chance. The Lord loves His people, and He wants to use us to reach them. He is faithful!

Love, Listen To Holy Ghost, Understand, And Action

I believe these four things are one of the essential keys to evangelism. We cannot do anything without having God's love bubbling out of us. I can usually tell when I am ministering to people out of my own strength because it does not produce a lot of fruit. Ministry becomes more works based.

The Lord always reminds me that I have left my first love when I try to minister out of my own strength. It's so important to be madly in love with Jesus, spending time in His presence. Then, when we come out of His presence His love is poured out to others.

Secondly, we need to listen while we minister to someone. Most of the time, people will pour their hearts out to us, and we need to listen to what they are saying. While they are talking, I have learned to listen to them, and often Holy Ghost will give me direction on how to pray. That is where understanding comes in. We need the Holy Ghost's wisdom and knowledge for every situation. Often, while praying for someone, the Lord will give us words of wisdom or words of knowledge to encourage the person.

Also, Holy Ghost may provide us with words of correction. Specifically, I had a young man I was praying for, and the Holy Ghost gave me a word for him. The Lord told me to tell him that he was heading for destruction if he did not change his associations. In Proverbs, the word tells us bad company corrupts morals.

It broke my heart, hearing later that he did not take the advice of the Lord and ended up in jail. I pray that he will give his heart to the Lord in prison. God loves him. Now, this brings me to the word, "act". The Holy Spirit will always give you direction to have the person act on what you have heard from the Holy Ghost. It is an opportunity for repentance and for prayer for them to give their life back to Jesus. The Lord is always there with open arms wanting His children to come home through repentance. He is a merciful God!

Chapter 11

Types of
Outreaches and Testimonies

Cross Ministry

This is one of my favorites! I have carried crosses at different times and seen others do this kind of ministry, but something changed when my mentor Evangelist Joel Crumpton taught me this. I remember us walking down the streets of downtown Atlanta with the cross. We were passing out tracks and talking to folks. We were sowing and watering, as I spoke about earlier.

Joel stopped us and said this to us, "Do not try to speak to another person. Instead, he said to pass out tracts as we walk. We will pray, asking the Lord to send us people to come up to us and ask us why we are carrying the cross." We prayed and did as he said. I was amazed! We had divine appointment after divine appointment for the rest of the day. People were coming up to us, asking us why we were carrying the cross.

This type of evangelism is so prophetic. Person after person would come up to us and ask us why we were carrying the cross. Joel would say, "We have been looking for you. We just prayed for you to come ask us that question," and then he would share the gospel. I use this method all the time. It is so much easier when God sends the people to you. The Lord has already prepared their hearts to receive. Here are a couple of testimonies from some of the cross outreaches.

Atlanta, Georgia

My son John and I had a great time evangelizing on downtown Atlanta's streets with all our incredible friends. We had a team of folks hit the streets led by Joel and Pat Crumpton. The Lord always uses them to stir a hunger in me for lost souls and for folks to be healed.

We prayed earlier for the Lord to draw folks to the cross and ask us why we are carrying the cross. A man named Christopher came and told us we were doing an incredible thing. I could not let him go! The Lord had me speak to him. I told him that we had just prayed for him, and he was our divine appointment. The Lord filled my words, and the next thing we knew, Christopher was weeping and giving his life to Jesus! Praise You, Lord, for one more soul written in the Lamb's book of life.

Friendship And Dyersburg, Tennessee

Wow! My son John and I had a wonderful time in Tennessee. We attended a Minister's Conference lead by Apostle Frost at Emmanuel Christian Fellowship. We had a chance to carry the cross at a park in Dyersburg with Jacob Laster. The Lord did quick work, and we walked into a divine appointment with a precious lady wearing a Trump shirt.

The Lord gave us all kinds of words of knowledge for her. Here is her testimony! "I met these three gentlemen at the Dyersburg Park today, and all three prayed for me, so blessed, divine appointment! God will find you wherever you are."

Door To Door/Panera Bread Ministry

Panera bread ministry is amazing. I had a friend who received Panera Bread every Monday night. Panera Bread does not use any preservatives in its bread, so they give all their leftovers away. It was on my friend Evangelist Warren Galvin's heart to go door to door with the bread. We would knock on the door, and we would give them a bag of bread and ask the people in the home if they needed any prayer. We have had so many testimonies from this outreach that I do not have enough time to share all of them, but I will share a few with you. We have learned that it is so much easier to have something to give when you go door to door to share the gospel. It is an ice breaker. Even if they do not want the bread, folks are usually open to prayer. Here are a couple of testimonies!

Amanda

In December of 2017, Evangelist Warren Galvin and I knocked on Amanda's door several times, and there was no answer. As we were about to walk away, she answered the door. We gave her a bag of Panera Bread and talked to her about salvation and the Holy Spirit's Baptism. Amanda had never heard the gospel before. Who would have thought that there are still people who have never heard the gospel in America? Amanda gave her life to the Lord and got filled in the Holy Spirit right on her front porch. Warren also took her through a time of deliverance. Amanda shared her testimony on Facebook Live, and it went viral. Amanda, with excitement, said that she had never experienced anything like the Holy Spirit and had gone through many avenues to get free from drugs and alcohol. Amanda experienced God's incredible presence right on her front porch. She has never been the same and got water baptized shortly after. All the glory goes to King Jesus!

Antoinette Hartley

This testimony is incredible! In March of 2017, the team was distributing Panera Bread at the Oakwood Terrace apartments. The Holy Spirit led me to knock on a couple of doors. I knocked on the upstairs door, and there was no answer. Then I went downstairs and knocked on Antoinette's door. I heard a soft voice coming from the apartment. She told me that she was in an accident and it was hard for her to go to the door. I told her that I was from Freedom Church and that I had a Panera Bread bag to give to her. She opened the door, and she was in a walker.

Kaye Newcombe saw her open the door and came to help me pray for her. We asked to pray for her healing. Antoinette told us that she had been a Sunday school teacher for many years. Her countenance shined as she showed us her teaching material and pictures of her children. She needed healing in her body to get back to these precious children. We prayed for Antoinette, and I remember her walking around some without her walker. The Lord was healing her, and we praised God and moved on to another apartment.

We Were Amazed!

A few weeks later, we were getting ready to leave Oakwood Terrace after a fabulous time of outreach, and I heard this voice. You are the man! You are the man! I went up to this lady, and it turned out that it was Antoinette Hartley. She was up and moving around. She told me that she had been trying to hunt me down. She wanted to say that the Lord was healing her, and she was now back teaching her children. The team prayed for the Lord to finish the work God started in her. Praise the Lord for His faithfulness! May the Lord continue to bless my precious friend Antoinette! Please pray for her to lead many more children to the Lord!

Treasure Hunts

By far, treasure hunts are one of my favorite ways to reach the lost. It is so much fun! The method was taught to me by my mentor Evangelist Joel Crumpton; he learned the method from the book called the *Ultimate Treasure Hunt* by Kevin Dedmon.

Here is the method Joel taught me. You get a team together, and on a three-by-five card, you write "location, name, appearance, need, and unusual" leaving a space after each clue. We would then pray and ask Holy Spirit to give us three to five things for each clue. Then we would give everyone a few minutes to write down the clues. We would go over our clues together and then re-lease teams into the city to find the clues.

I loved it because all our clues came together like a piece in a puzzle. The team truly is the body of Christ putting our pieces to-gether to find the lost soul that was on the Father's heart for that day. We have had so many divine appointments doing treasure hunts that I could take all day sharing them with you. Here are some testimonies from our treasure hunts.

Kenny Saved And Filled With The Holy Ghost

As soon as I got back from a Mexico trip, I received a message from my evangelist friend Joel Crumpton that the Picayune evan-gelism weekend date was changed. Joel believed that God moved the date because there were folks there that hung in the balance of eternity. I knew right away that I had to rearrange everything to be there. The Lord was about to do some amazing things!

That Friday night in Picayune, Brother Joel taught us about the power of proclamation, and on Saturday, we had a treasure hunt. The Lord had given me some clues, but my main ones were a snake tattoo or tattoo, Wal-Mart, and the grocery department. We walked into Wal-Mart and decided to head to the grocery department. John Guidry immediately was drawn to a man who had tattoos and said to me that we needed to pray for him. I went with him, and John engaged the man in conversation.

The man's name was Kenny. John asked Kenny if we could pray for him. I talked to him some, and one of the girls went to get Joel. Joel came, spoke to him about his salvation, and Kenny got down on his knees and gave his life to the Lord right there in the beer aisle in Wal-Mart. Joel also talked to him about the Holy Ghost's Baptism, and he received the Baptism of the Holy Ghost, as well. It turned out that Kenny was about to buy beer, and something told him to buy water instead. We know now that it was the Holy Ghost, and He had sent messengers to lead Kenny back to Jesus.

Amazing Treasure Hunt Testimony

We had many treasure hunt teams going out throughout the week, and the Lord did amazing things! We put the team together by location. One team member, Ginger Keating, kept getting a clue to go to a nursing home on Davis Highway. Other team members were getting clues to go to that same area, and the word "life" was one of the clues. I asked Ginger if she could connect us with a nursing home, and she could not. We debated where to go to lunch before going out on our treasure hunt, and we all agreed upon Simply Greek. When all of us got to Simply Greek we discovered that a local nursing home had taken their residents there to eat and was in the process of loading the people back into the bus.

We had an opportunity to pray for several of them, and I got on the bus to preach. I shared with them that they may feel all alone, but Jesus had never forgotten about them, that He loves them, and had sent us there to pray for them. Here is the kicker! The nursing home's name was Life Care Center! We were in the right place at the right time, and we had so many divine appointments at Simply Greek we could not leave! Our Lord is amazing!

Treasure Hunt Pensacola, Florida

We went over all our clues before the team went to the Mall! I was walking to the bathroom and saw a girl with bright red hair. I remembered that someone had a clue about someone with red hair. Team member Aaron Brewer had it on his card, and we went over to talk to her. Aaron shared his clues with her, and she immediately started to cry. Aaron and several of us had prophetic words for her, and she needed emotional healing from unforgiveness! We lead her in a prayer to let the people go that had hurt her! Team member Nicole Segars prayed for the red-haired woman's friend whose neck was hurting and she received immediate healing! God is so amazing! Jesus gets all the glory!

Flea Market Outreach

I highly recommend this type of outreach to every church. This outreach idea came from one of our students, Sally Patterson, during our evangelism class at King's Way Church. At the end of the course, we planned to do an outreach, so I asked the class for some suggestions. Sally Patterson suggested we go to the flea market. I immediately knew in my spirit that we should do this. I had gone to the flea market a few times before and walked around to pray for folks, but this idea allowed us to get a booth and put up a sign saying "Free Prayer, Free Healing, Free Bibles, etc." We would have people sign up for two-hour shifts throughout the day to serve. The Lord has done so many amazing things throughout this outreach that I cannot share them all, but here a few testimonies from the outreaches.

Pensacola Flea Market Ministry

Words cannot describe what happened one day at our T&W Flea Market Outreach! We had several churches involved! Many divine appointments! We had two girls from Crown Church lead in worship! We had folks give their hearts to Jesus, and we got to pray for many people! The Lord also connected us with many folks from the body of Christ! Here is just one of the testimonies that happened. This precious girl came up to me and said, please pray for me. She said she was in pain! I told her that I had good news for her. The Kingdom of Heaven has come near her today! The team prayed for her, and we lead her to Jesus! She felt amazingly better! Praise to the Name of Jesus!

Flea Market Outreach Testimonies

This testimony is amazing! My wife Tami asked me if I could smell perfume. I said no and asked her if she was wearing any. She said, "No, the Holy Spirit is here." After that, Roy came to our booth broken and crying, asking for prayer. He told us that he had lost everything. Joe Sewell, my wife Tami, and I got to minister to him, lead him back to Jesus, and he received the Baptism of the Holy Ghost. All the glory goes to King Jesus!

I love this testimony. We were worshiping, and we had a gentleman stop at the booth across from us. Brother Dennis Godwin went to minister to him and called me over. The gentleman was from Honduras and knew no English. Several of our team members wanted to minister to the man but could not communicate with him. Dennis asked me about the church, All Nations House of Prayer, and we tried to look it up online to connect the man. Here is the kicker: around fifteen minutes later, the Lord sent us someone from that church to minister to him and invite him to their church! They decided to hang out with us to minister to more people! The Kingdom of Heaven is growing! Praise the Lord!

Children's Outreaches

Children's outreach opened to us through our Panera Bread Ministry. We would take bread into the Oakwood Terrace apartment complex and the children would welcome us and want to help pull our carts and pass out bread to the community. Immediately, I could feel the Lord's compassion for these children. I knew we needed to do something with these children, so we did.

Our team would go to the Oakwood Terrace playground area and love them. We played games with them, fed them, and gave them drinks, but most of all, we would sit down with them and teach them about Jesus and pray. You could feel in your heart that the Lord was pleased with what we were doing. Oakwood Terrace is one of the most challenging sections of town.

These children have a rough life. Drugs and shootings are rampant in their area, but it would brighten up their day when we would come. I remember one child crying, not wanting us to leave. The Lord was doing something special in their hearts. Here are a couple of testimonies from our children's outreaches. What a special time they have been!

Pensacola, Florida

Our children's outreach was so unique! We had two teams. Our friend, Fraga DaRosa held a soccer camp with the children at our favorite place, Oakwood Terrace. The children had so much fun. You know that you have an impact on the children when they are happy to see you come and sad to see you go. I enjoyed watching my son John and another friend from his soccer team from school help with this.

The presence of the Lord was wonderful! Fraga split the children into groups where they received Bible lessons from the amazing Youth Reach guys. Fraga then shared his testimony, and several of the children received the Lord that day. All praise goes to King Jesus!

Our second team was terrific, as well. They ministered to the more minor children with music, songs, games, and a Bible lesson. They even went on a parade around the park. What a significant blessing it was to see how happy these children were! We celebrated with them afterwards with oranges, rice crispy treats, and juice boxes. The children were wrapped in God's love.

Plasma Center Outreaches

These kinds of outreaches have been excellent! We park in the plasma center's parking lot and give out Subway lunches. Most folks who go to the plasma center are desperate due to significant financial needs. We give them lunch and ask them if they need prayer. We have a huge percentage of people that say yes. We share the gospel with them during prayer and lead them back to the Lord. Many of them receive healing and the baptism of the Holy Spirit, as well. The Lord loves the poor so much! Here are a few testimonies from our Plasma Center Outreaches.

Pensacola, Florida Plasma Center Outreaches

The Lord did so many amazing things in the Plasma Center parking lot. A precious man saw us, came over and we gave him lunch! Pastor John Walker and Evangelist Warren Galvin started ministering to him. The man's brother was driving in the parking lot, saw him, and jumped out of his truck! Both guys accepted the Lord and got the Holy Ghost! Jesus is Amazing!

A precious girl walked right up to us in the Plasma Center parking lot on Saturday. We asked if we could give her lunch and pray for her. She immediately hollered, "Yes, I need prayer!" After we started praying for her, she broke down and started crying. She shared how she was homeless and how she gave plasma to survive. The Lord touched her, and she gave her life to the Lord. Then, she got filled with the Holy Ghost! The Lord Jesus poured out His love on her! Pastor John Walker from Walls of Salvation Church was there with us, and we took down her information for him to follow up with her. She is so precious; please pray for her!

Homeless Outreach

The Lord opened this ministry up to us right when the COVID-19 pandemic hit. I had just come back from a trip to Mexico and had overcome many sicknesses. We were in lockdown for two weeks, so I was resting and praying. I will never forget the Lord's still small voice come into my spirit while praying. He asked me who was taking care of the homeless. I posted what I heard from God on Facebook, and one of my friends was going out to feed them, so I started helping. It turned out that every shelter and food pantry had shut down. The homeless were in desperate need. I remember one of the guys we fed said to us that people would not even roll down their windows to talk to them. We were able to provide for them and pray for them. The Lord was doing amazing work.

While feeding them, the Lord would show me the people's needs. One was that many of them needed tents. We were getting closer to the summer season where the rains would start coming in. These precious people would not have a covering, so the Lord gave me the heart to bless them with tents. Praise God, for the provision of the Lord! He is faithful! Here are a few testimonies from some of the homeless outreaches.

Homeless Outreach In Pensacola

It was such an honor to serve with Jon and Hayley Klover and Jonathan and Sarah Liechty to reach the homeless in Pensacola. We brought the homeless home cooked meals and hygiene bags. We loved hearing their stories and were able to pray with them and share the good news. Cindy, a homeless woman, gave her life to Jesus through this outreach. Praise the Lord! She is precious; please pray for her!

Homeless Outreach Testimonies Pensacola, FL

It is so unique that we were getting relationships with these precious folks in need on the streets of Pensacola. David needed healing for a skin condition he had suffered with for several weeks. The team prayed for him. I ran into him a couple of days later blessing him with a tent, and he told me that the skin condition had started clearing up. Praise God!

Missions

From a young age, I always had an interest in the nations of the world. I remember entering an essay contest in the fifth grade. I was looking at the prizes, and what sparked my interest was a globe. I would spin the ball and look at the nations, so I entered the contest to win it. It turned out that I did so well on the essay that I ended up winning a big dictionary. I remember being so disappointed that I did not win the globe.

This stuck with me my whole life. A few years ago, my half-sister Mandy bought me a globe which I now have in my room. I had no idea that the Lord would send me to many different nations to share the gospel, including our own country, the United States of America. Like I shared before, the Lord sent Tami and I to Pensacola, FL to go to Bible School. I will never forget the class graduation. This scripture has always stuck with me since that day, *"Ask of Me, and I will give you the nations for your inheritance and the uttermost parts of the earth for your possession."* (Psalm 2:8)

Our teachers and leaders would talk about the nations, and the hunger in my heart would burn for the lost and broken. I had no idea where the Lord would send me, but I knew that one day He would. The student body put money together and bought flags from many of the nations around the world. We surprised the faculty with them by walking down the aisle of our graduation with the song called, "You Said" by Hillsong in the background. You could sense the Lord's presence in that meeting. God had marked every student with His heart to reach the nations with the gospel. The nations burned in my heart.

I had no idea what the Lord would do in my life and which nation he would call me to. I had no idea that he would have me travel to several countries, and He continues to add to it. I believe the Lord loves to test us to see if we are faithful in a little, and He makes us ruler over much.

I remember sitting in a Hispanic church service one time. My friend Fabian had come back from Iraq to preach there. I was sitting there enjoying the worship in Spanish and I loved the hunger of the people. In a still small voice, the Lord spoke to me and said that I did not have to go to the nations to reach the countries. He said the nations are here! I was like, wow! He was calling me to start where I was. I lived in Pensacola, so he wanted me to start here, and I have not stopped since.

Missions To Mexico And Abroad

After the Lord had reconnected me with my good friend Missionary Richard Davis from Bible school, he introduced me to Pastor Abraham Javine to start going to Mexico. We had taken toys there for the precious people in Nuevo Laredo. Pastor Ray Rendon Jr. took us around to visit the families, and we gave out the toys. The Lord was setting me up. Here is the testimony of what happened!

December 23, 2014 - Jasmine, The Girl That Gave Me The Chocolate Ball

I was changed after returning from that powerful time in Mexico. I will never forget the little girl named Jasmine that gave me a chocolate ball. Our team was out visiting poor families and delivering toys to the children. This little girl was so happy to receive a gift from us that she ran back to her room and got chocolate balls for everyone. She wanted to make sure Richard, Pastor Javine, and I would have something for Christmas. This act touched my heart so deeply that I could not eat the chocolate ball. I wanted to take it home, but it melted in my pocket. This act by this precious girl will forever be in my heart!

The Lord would use Jasmine to melt my heart for the children that we have gone back to visit many times, bringing toys, gifts, and supplies to these precious people in the Colonia. God was now adding to my assignments. You see, my friend when we are faithful in a little, He will give us more. He continues to add more and more assignments in U.S. cities as well as places in Mexico and Costa Rica. The Lord has been faithful to provide for every assignment. The Lord loves the lost and wants no one to perish. Open your heart! He may be sending you next. I pray you answer the call to go. You can do it!

Chapter 12

Revelations for the Lost

Reach My Bride Dream

I can remember this dream like it was yesterday. In the dream, the Lord took me to a rich school, and there was a rich girl there. I could see how happy she was and how content she was in the school. It was a comfortable feeling. I started feeling like I was content with the school, and I felt like I was falling asleep. Suddenly, the Lord took me to another school. It was poor. Everything was old, broken down, and the playground was old, as well. It did not even look like any children had been there for years.

Suddenly, a little girl came to my attention. I could see her clothes were dirty and had holes in them. She was poor, and my heart went out to her. I wanted to help her with everything that I had. I heard the Lord ask me a question. I am giving you a choice. Would you be content with this rich school, or would you be willing to risk everything to reach this poor little girl in the poor school? I knew what He was asking, and I said yes in the dream. I knew he was asking me to get His bride and bring them home. Since that dream, I have not looked back.

Reinhard Bonnke Video - Lost At Sea

When I woke up from this dream, I told my wife. She immediately reminded me of a Reinhard Bonnke film called "Lost at Sea" concerning reaching lost souls. I was amazed that this story was like my dream. The story was about a pleasure boat with passengers having a great time representing the church. They had such a great time they started losing their heart for the people that were drowning outside of their boat.

You see, the ship is a lifeboat, not a pleasure boat at all. When the people came to recruit the folks on the boat to rescue the ones drowning outside, only a handful would answer the call. The others had been distracted by the pleasures of what was inside the ship.

The Lord designed us to be a lifeboat, and when we lose sight of that reality, we become just like the world. We become like any other worldly club. When there is no outflow to go after lost souls, we become stagnant Christians. The Lord wants us to be a lifeboat.

Point 1 - We Make Excuses - We're Too Comfortable!

Luke 14:15-24 says, *"Now when one of those who sat at the table with Him heard these things, he said to Him, "Blessed is he who shall eat bread in the kingdom of God!"*

Then He said to him, "A certain man gave a great supper and invited many, and sent his servant at supper time to say to those who were invited, 'Come, for all things are now ready.' But they all with one accord began to make excuses. The first said to him, 'I have bought a piece of ground, and I must go and see it. I ask you to have me excused.' And another said, 'I have bought five yoke of oxen, and I am going to test them. I ask you to have me excused.'

Still another said, 'I have married a wife, and therefore I cannot come.' So that servant came and reported these things to his master. Then the master of the house, being angry, said to his servant, 'Go out quickly into the streets and lanes of the city, and bring in here the poor and the maimed and the lame and the blind.'

And the servant said, 'Master, it is done as you commanded, and still there is room.' Then the master said to the servant, 'Go out into the highways and hedges, and compel them to come in, that my house may be filled. For I say to you that none of those men who were invited shall taste my supper."

Let us stop making excuses. The Lord's heart is for everyone to come to the great supper, and he wants to use us to reach them. I say yes, Lord send me!

Point 2- Everyone Is Invited, But Not Everyone Comes!

We Must Have The Wedding Garment On! (The Blood Of Jesus)

Matthew 22:1-14 says, *"And Jesus answered and spoke to them again by parables and said: "The kingdom of heaven is like a certain king who arranged a marriage for his son and sent out his servants to call those who were invited to the wedding; and they were not willing to come.*

Again, he sent out other servants, saying, 'Tell those who are invited, "See, I have prepared my dinner; my oxen and fatted cattle are killed, and all things are ready. Come to the wedding."

But they made light of it and went their ways, one to his own farm, another to his business. And the rest seized his servants, treated them spitefully, and killed them.

But when the King heard about it, he was furious. And he sent out his armies, destroyed those murderers, and burned up their city. Then he said to his servants, 'The wedding is ready, but those who were invited were not worthy. Therefore, go into the high-

ways, and as many as you find, invite to the wedding.' So those servants went out into the highways and gathered together all whom they found, both bad and good. And the wedding hall was filled with guests.

"But when the King came in to see the guests, he saw a man there who did not have on a wedding garment. So he said to him, 'Friend, how did you come in here without a wedding garment?' And he was speechless. Then the King said to the servants, 'Bind him hand and foot, take him away, and cast him into outer darkness; there will be weeping and gnashing of teeth.'

"For many are called, but few are chosen."

The Lord showed me that the only way we get in is through the blood of Jesus. That wedding garment represents His blood, and we must go get the people and lead them to Jesus. Also, there are lost souls even in the congregation, and we must reach them, as well. May we not just assume that while we share the gospel in a church setting, everyone is born again. We must give them an opportunity to come to Jesus. The Lord loves them!

Point 3 - It's Going To Be Glorious

Revelation 19:1-10 says, *"After these things I heard a loud voice of a great multitude in heaven, saying, "Alleluia! Salvation and glory and honor and power belong to the Lord our God! For true and righteous are His judgments, because He has judged the great harlot who corrupted the earth with her fornication; and He has avenged on her the blood of His servants shed by her."*

Again, they said, "Alleluia! Her smoke rises up forever and ever!" And the twenty-four elders and the four living creatures fell down and worshiped God who sat on the throne, saying, "Amen! Alleluia!" Then a voice came from the throne, saying, "Praise our God, all you His servants and those who fear Him, both small and great!"

And I heard, as it were, the voice of a great multitude, as the sound of many waters and as the sound of mighty thunderings, saying, "Alleluia! For the Lord God Omnipotent reigns! Let us be glad and rejoice and give Him glory, for the marriage of the lamb has come, and His wife has made herself ready." And to her it was granted to be arrayed in fine linen, clean and bright, for the fine linen is the righteous acts of the saints."

Then he said to me, "Write: 'Blessed are those who are called to the marriage supper of the Lamb!'" And he said to me, "These are the true sayings of God." And I fell at his feet to worship him. But he said to me, "See that you do not do that! I am your fellow servant, and of your brethren who have the testimony of Jesus. Worship God! For the testimony of Jesus is the spirit of prophecy."

What a wonderful time this will be! I have only had a glimpse of what the Lamb's marriage supper is going to be like. I remember waiting in line for the Brownsville Revival. Christians had come from all over the world to meet with Jesus. People would line up outside of the church by the early morning hours, hungry to meet with Jesus. I remember the Lord touching us in the line while we waited, worshipping, and praying together. Later in the evening, the wait was over, and thousands started pouring into the church sanctuary. Lindell Cooley, the worship leader, would come out and hit the keys, and thousands of believers hungry to meet Jesus would let out a scream crying out His name. My ears would ring from the noise, but I was overjoyed, so hungry for God that it did not bother me. The Lord's presence would come to touch us all, but the marriage supper of the Lamb is going to be like that on steroids. Billions upon billions of believers throughout the ages coming together, cheering Alleluia, the Lord omnipotent reigns. It's going to be glorious!

The Cloud Of Witnesses

Hebrews 12:1-2 says, *"Therefore we also, since we are surrounded by so great a cloud of witnesses, let us lay aside every weight, and the sin which so easily ensnares us, and let us run with endurance the race that is set before us, looking unto Jesus, the author and finisher of our faith, who for the joy that was set before Him endured the cross, despising the shame, and has sat down at the right hand of the throne of God."*

One day, I remember praying in my car and the Lord asking me with a still small voice, "What do I see?" I closed my eyes, and all I could see was people's faces in giant bubbles clapping and cheering. I knew in my spirit that this was the great cloud of witnesses cheering for us. We will all be together one day telling stories of the goodness of God. It's going to be glorious when we're all together.

Dream From A Friend

My Intercessor friend Judi Schultz shared this dream with me. I am only going to share part of it, but this changed my life forever, and I hope it does yours as well. The Lord took her to heaven, and an angel led her to a large room. She said she saw people outside waiting to get in and asked the angel why they were not coming in.

The angel sat her down at a table all alone. She knew that this was the Lamb's marriage supper and was trying to figure out why she was sitting alone. The angel said to her, "Remember the people outside that were waiting to come in? They are the people assigned to you to bring them to the feast." When I read that, I broke down and cried. I felt the weightiness of it in a good way that the Lord would entrust me to help rescue the lost and bring them home. You see, my friends, the Lord has people assigned only to us to lead them home, and these will be the saints sitting with us at the marriage supper of the Lamb. It's going to be amazing!

We Were Born For Such A Time As This!

Two years ago, I was in one of the most life-changing meetings of my life. I was attending the School of Evangelism at Christ for All Nations (CFAN). Daniel Kolenda showed us a video of Reinhard Bonnke sharing his heart about God's calling on his life. He shared about the dream he had of the Lord washing Africa with the blood of Jesus. Reinhard was wresting with a choice. His sending organization wanted to pull him off the field, and he wrestled with that choice. In prayer, Reinhard wrestled with the Lord, and the Lord spoke to him, saying, "If you drop the vision of a blood--washed Africa, I will drop you!" He made up his mind, typed his resignation, and obeyed the Lord; since that time, hundreds of millions of souls have come into the kingdom. Praise the Lord for Reinhard, an obedient vessel.

I remember Kathryn Kuhlman, who was used mightily by God in the 1960's and 1970's as a healing evangelist. She would always tell people that she was not God's first choice. A couple of men had not accepted what God had called them to do, so the mantle came to Kathryn, and she accepted the call.

Daniel Kolenda preached on Esther's story and it's interesting that I am remembering this during the season of Purim. The children of Israel would read the book of Esther out loud every year to remember the deliverance of the Lord. Most of us know the story. Haman hated the Jews and plotted to wipe the whole population off the face of the earth, but the plot got defeated by the obedience of one amazing woman. Daniel pointed out this scripture to us, and here are some things I learned from his teaching at the School of Evangelism.

Esther 4:13-14 says, *"And Mordecai told them to answer Esther: "Do not think in your heart that you will escape in the King's palace any more than all the other Jews. For if you remain completely silent at this time, relief and deliverance will arise for the Jews from another place, but you and your father's house will perish. Yet who knows whether you have come to the kingdom for such a time as this?"*

Esther was extremely poor and was living in the house of her uncle. She suddenly was picked to be queen, so she goes from rags to riches. She goes into the palace of the King, and things get comfortable. Suddenly there comes a choice to obey God. Her uncle wanted her to go to the King and plead for her people. She wrestled with the choice. A person could only go before the King unless he summoned them by the scepter, according to the law; the punishment was death. What could happen? She could lose everything, even her life.

Daniel Kolenda shared Mordecai's sobering statement that if Esther did not obey God, surely the Lord would raise someone else to deliver Israel, but she and her household would perish. I felt the weight of that on my life. Every CFAN student hit the floor under repentance, screaming, and wailing. In my heart, I was overwhelmed with the fact that God could replace the calling on my life with somebody else if I didn't obey. The Lord was doing significant work in my life. It was a valley of decision moment for me. I got up from that floor, changed, and committed to obeying God. You see, my friends, every one of us God has called specially and uniquely. I pray for the Lord to give you a revelation of His calling and that you would say yes.

You see, we are not our own. The Lord repurchased us with a price; he wants all of us to get a hold of His heart and reach the lost. He has people assigned to you and me to bring to the Lamb's marriage supper. Esther obeyed God, and the rest is history. Through Esther, the Lord stopped Haman's plot, and the King put forth a decree to help save the Jews' lives. We seek the Lord, pray, and get so filled up with His love and compassion that we go out by His direction to rescue the lost. What an incredible time to be alive! We were born for such a time as this!

An Effectual Door

Once when praying, I received a vision of a door. I cannot shake it. I saw the door. A door that probably would have existed around the time of Moses. It had blood covering the entrance. I remembered how the Dark Angel passed by the Israelites homes during

Moses' time. The Lord released a judgment on the firstborn males. Every firstborn son would die unless blood was on the doorposts. The Holy Spirit spoke to my heart that there is still judgment. Because of sin, there is judgment, but Jesus paid for it with His very own blood. John 3:18 says, *"He who believes in Him is not condemned; but he who does not believe is condemned already, because he has not believed in the name of the only begotten Son of God."*

Jesus is the Lamb that was slain before the foundation of the earth. Unless we receive what, He paid for, we are already judged and will be separated for eternity. An effectual door is opened to us, but there are many adversaries. The devil wants us not to receive what Jesus paid for and throws out many obstacles. We must walk through that door of safety. The blood of Jesus covers a multitude of sins. We must go all the way in.

If one of the Israelite's first-born sons even had a small part of his body outside the door of safety, he would have been killed. The Lord wants all our heart, not just part of it. We must be born again! We must surrender everything! We leave our selfish desires behind and give Jesus our life! Full surrender! Not my will but yours be done, Jesus!

141

Matthew 16:24-28 says, *"Then Jesus said to His disciples, 'If anyone desires to come after Me, let him deny himself, and take up his cross, and follow Me. For whoever desires to save his life will lose it, but whoever loses his life for My sake will find it. For what profit is it to a man if he gains the whole world, and loses his own soul? Or what will a man give in exchange for his soul? For the Son of Man will come in the glory of His Father with His angels, and then He will reward each according to his works. Assuredly, I say to you, there are some standing here who shall not taste death till they see the Son of Man coming in His kingdom.'"*

If we choose this world, we only have what this world will offer which is emptiness. Your reward is only really what you can get in this life, and the Lord lets us choose that if we want, but in the end, that choice separates us from the Lord for eternity. I cannot fathom it. I know that there is hell, eternal flames, a Lake of Fire, and all those things plus being separated from God for eternity. You may never have another chance. The chances are over!

The decision to give your life to Jesus is now! The blood of Jesus is on the mercy seat. He has made a way for you and me. He intercedes at the right hand of the Father so that no one would perish, but he has given the final choice for us to make! I hope you make the decision today! Just get on your knees and cry out to Him. He will hear you. Turn from sin and give your life to King Jesus. All of you! Make Him Lord and Savior! Every part of you must be behind the door covered in the blood! He is waiting for you with open arms! Do not wait another moment! It could be your last chance! Take it now!

Biography

Rudy Waters serves as the President of *Go and Declare Inc.,* a ministry established in February 2016. He has a tremendous heart to win souls and make disciples by spreading the Gospel of Jesus Christ through ministering to the needs of communities around the world. Rudy received An Associate Degree in Practical Ministry from the Brownsville Revival School of Ministry on December 16, 2000, in Pensacola, Florida.

He has been an ordained minister of the gospel for six years and is authorized and commissioned to exercise and perform all functions, rites, and ceremonies of the Christian faith and gospel by the authority of Fellowship for International Revival Evangelism, Inc. in Concord, North Carolina.

Made in the USA
Coppell, TX
26 February 2024

29324584R00090